Branding
Miss G___

Third Wave Feminists
and the Media

MICHELLE MILLER

SUMACH
PRESS

WOMEN'S ISSUES PUBLISHING PROGRAM

SERIES EDITOR BETH MCAULEY

LIBRARY AND ARCHIVES CANADA CATALOGUING IN PUBLICATION

Miller, Michelle, 1981-
Branding Miss G__ : third wave feminists and the media /
Michelle Miller.

Includes bibliographical references and index.
ISBN 978-1-894549-72-1

1. Miss G_ Project for Equity in Education. 2. Feminism and mass media—Ontario. 3. Mass media and public opinion—Ontario. 4. Educational equalization—Ontario. I. Title.

HQ1155.M45 2008   305.42'09713   C2008-901795-1

Copyright © 2008 Michelle Miller

Edited by Beth McAuley
Designed by Liz Martin

Sumach Press acknowledges the support of the Canada Council for the Arts and the Ontario Arts Council for our publishing program. We acknowledge the financial support of the Government of Canada through the Book Publishing Industry Development Program (BPIDP) for our publishing activities.

Printed and bound in Canada

Published by
SUMACH PRESS
1415 Bathurst Street #202
Toronto ON Canada
M5R 3H8

sumachpress@on.aibn.com
www.sumachpress.com

For all the amazing women in my life.

CONTENTS

Acknowledgements 9

Introduction:
Launching the Brand
11

Chapter 1
Lobbying Like Ladies
39

Chapter 2
The Third Wave, Femininity and Public Performance
65

Chapter 3
Packaging a (non)Feminist Image
93

Chapter 4
Tracking Media Representations
123

Chapter 5
From Branding to Political Action
157

Appendix
Script: No More Miss Nice G__! 169

References 177

Index 188

ACKNOWLEDGEMENTS

First and foremost, I'd like to thank Dr. Rebecca Coulter whose advice, support and involvement has been vital to this process from day one. I truly couldn't have done this without you and I am so grateful to have you as a teacher, a mentor and a friend. Thanks to the girls from Miss G__: Sarah, Dilani, Sheetal and Lara, as well as Laurel and Jenna. Thanks for your time and energy, for the incredible work you've done for the Project and especially for being so open minded to this critique. Thank you for helping me to prove that, in this movement, taking a step back and critiquing our approaches to activism can be a positive and necessary thing. Thanks also to Drs. Wayne Martino and Marianne Larsen for your help when the seed for this book was my MEd thesis.

Thanks to my partner, Rachel, for being so patient with me throughout this process and for making literally hundreds of cups of coffee, and to my mom for thinking I had a book in me.

Of course, thanks to my editor, Beth McAuley, and everyone from Sumach Press for all of their incredible help in making this book possible.

Introduction:

LAUNCHING THE BRAND

Because the current curriculum has no way of examining the complex ways in which sexism, racism, heterosexism and other forms of discrimination are intimately related and linked.
— The Miss G__ Project for Equity in Education (2007c)

IN THE FALL OF 2005, ONTARIO'S MINISTRY OF EDUCATION OFFICES began to receive hundreds of bright pink postcards emblazoned with the face of a mysterious and cheeky-looking young woman with glasses and a cute bob. The back of each postcard began "We need a women's studies course in Ontario's curriculum because ..." and ended with an anecdote about the sender's own high school experience, past or present. These postcards, which were part of a lobbying campaign introduced by the Miss G__ Project for Equity in Education, sent a very strong message to MPPs that a women's studies course on the official curriculum was important, not just to special interest activist groups, but to ordinary people of all ages, different sexes and social positions. Cards came in from high school, college and university students, parents, school system alumni, teachers, union officials and myriad others. Miss G__ members distributed these postcards at lobbying events and through feminist groups in several cities, and while everyone who participated in the campaign agreed on the need for this sort of course, every person had a different, though related, reason for wanting it. Some

Branding Miss G__

participants reached for theory, "because we go through our mandatory formal education careers without ever encountering a critical study of gender construction and socialization, and most importantly, its implications," while some went from their gut, "because [violence against women is a worldwide problem and women using] pepper spray won't solve the problem."

The Miss G__ steering committee created these postcards with several strategies in mind. First, by allowing individual participants to explain their own interests in a course that would address gender, they could emphasize that their campaigns included and reflected the needs of a variety of people, working from separate and related experiences. By placing the project's logo — the face of the historical unnamed Miss G__ front and centre — they hoped to position themselves as the go-to group on the issue of promoting gender equity in education, creating some consistency in the effort and presenting an organized, well-conceived effort. By making the cards bright pink, they ensured the cards would be immediately recognizable as they came in, and nearly impossible to ignore. Of course, visibility was not the only reason the group chose pink as their colour.

Throughout their written correspondence with politicians, Miss G__ has maintained a consistent image of being feminine good-time girls. The steering committee of Miss G__ believes that their lighthearted, cute and feminine image initially gained them support, because by using it they could avoid alienating potential supporters at Queen's Park by seeming "too political." Of course, the concern associated with this was that by seeming light-hearted, they might also come across as being not-serious and not-capable. They considered this a sort of "Trojan horse" strategy, with which they could surprise MPPs by being competent, serious and well prepared in meetings, while being fun and frivolous in the press and in their correspondence.

Miss G__ steering committee members Sheetal Rawal, Sarah Ghabrial, Dilani Mohan and Lara Shdorkoff have been very explicit about this "Trojan Containment" strategy, explaining it

INTRODUCTION: LAUNCHING THE BRAND

this way:

>*Ghabrial:* Part of our public image has been young and fun and playful and coy and ...
>
>*Rawal:* ... coquettish.
>
>*Ghabrial:* But then in meetings and things, when we actually sit down and have our meetings with ministry officials, we are obviously serious, and it's interesting. I mean, I think in a lot of ways they don't expect us to be well versed and knowledgeable and serious about what we're talking about; it kind of works; it's like a Trojan horse.
>
>*Rawal:* Trojan containment!
>
>*Ghabrial:* Yeah, it's like we come in as like fun girls with croquet mallets but ...
>
>*Rawal:* ... we want a course!
>
>*Ghabrial:* And we come in with all of this documentation, and we're well spoken and prepared, and I think that's part of the advantage.

This "Trojan Containment" strategy is smart, but only if it is successful. Groups like Miss G__, which attempt to appear harmless and apolitical in order to gain the government's attention without alienating them, should be aware that this strategy may interfere with their ability to gain the face-to-face meetings they need to prove themselves as an organized effort. Groups also need to be aware that for this kind of strategy to be effective, politicians must buy into it, walking a fine line between being interested in the project and believing that the group is less politically effective and organized than it actually is. More troublesome is the possibility that by appearing apolitical in lobbying, any successes that the group achieves will be limited to the adoption of an apolitical version of their proposed course of action.

The Miss G__ Project's faux-apolitical approach to lobbying is consistent with a wider movement in feminism in Canada and the United States. Organizing under the banner of feminism's "third wave," many groups of young women are working as feminists while simultaneously embracing a version of femininity that many see as being inconsistent with feminism's supposedly more political second wave. While this strategy is hotly contested by feminists of all stripes, there has only been one prior synthesis of the importance of image to feminist lobbying in Ontario or Canada, Barbara Freeman's (2001) *The Satellite Sex: The Media and Women's Issues in English Canada, 1966–1971*. At this time, it seems to be greatly important to take a critical look at image-related strategies in contemporary feminism in order to see if so-called third wave approaches to lobbying are effective in gaining positive media and political attention.

Too little research has been done on the work of young Canadian feminists within and outside the third wave of feminism. There are, of course, exceptions to this rule. The journal *Canadian Woman Studies* acknowledged in its 2001 special issue "Young Women, Feminists, Activists, Grrls" that a feminist movement for young women does exist in Canada. The popular feminist magazine *Herizons* devotes some space to the work and achievements of young feminists in its monthly issues. The teen magazine *Shameless* focuses on the social, political and cultural lives of young women, many of whom self-define as feminists. Many third wave texts occur outside of academia, taking the form of anthologies of personal essays, either original or previously posted on weblogs (blogs) or in zines. A zine is a do-it-yourself (DIY) magazine independently published in small runs, usually photocopied, stapled or sewn together; a blog can be best understood as an online zine. To this point, one third wave feminist anthology has been published in Canada: Alyson Mitchell, Lisa Bryn Rundle and Lara Karaian's (2001) *Turbo Chicks: Talking Young Feminisms*. Otherwise, Canadian third wave works have only been available through non-mainstream publishers and difficult to collect (Steenbergen 1999, 98). Much of my information about third wave feminism comes from these diverse types of non-academic sources, especially third wave apologetics such as Jennifer Baumgardner and Amy Richards' (2000) *Manifesta! Young Women, Feminism and the Future*, Rebecca Walker's (1995) *To Be Real: Telling the Truth and Changing the Face of Feminism*, and

INTRODUCTION: LAUNCHING THE BRAND ·

Leslie Heywood and Jennifer Drake's (1997) *Third Wave Agenda: Being Feminist, Doing Feminism*. This emphasis on anthologizing third wave writings allows the activists and theorists who make up the third wave to define it through their own experiences.

Academia suffers from a lack of work on women in general and feminists in particular. Judy Rebick (2005) believes that "radical uppity women make people in power nervous, so they are disappeared from history whenever possible" (xiii). Young feminists are even more invisible in popular feminist and scholarly discourse, leading Rebick and Roach (1996) to argue further that "the women's movement has not paid enough attention to the needs and voices of young women" (3). In 2005, Roberta Hamilton's *Gendering the Vertical Mosaic* criticized the mainstream media for perpetuating the myth that feminism is dead (39). However, in her chapter on the women's movement(s) in Canada, she acknowledges the possible existence of a third wave of Canadian feminism in less than a half page, under the title "Third-wave feminism? Post-feminism? Anti-feminism?" (69). Hamilton's reluctance to write about a third wave of feminism, or the work of young feminists at all, lends credence to the popular reactionary claims she disparages, contributing to what Debi Morgan (1995) sees as a dangerous cycle, wherein "because little is written about young women due to their marginalization, few young women identify with or engage with the feminist movement. This leads to little research, academic study or recording, which in turn leads to further marginalization of young women" (135).

Feminism and young people are similarly disparaged in the press. The phrase "feminism is dead" was printed in *Time* magazine at least 119 times between 1969 and 1998 (Steinem 2003, 109–110). The media also circulates the notions that "young people are lazy and apathetic" (Kitch 2003, 192; Steenbergen 1999, 66; Rundle 1998, 24) and that "the goals of feminism have been achieved" (Morgan 2003a, xvii; *Briarpatch* Editorial Collective 2006, 2; Freeman 2001, 1). These backlash claims are media constructions, intended to demonize both feminists and youth to create the false sense that equity has been achieved and feminism is no longer necessary. Often,

Branding Miss G___

these claims are made by young, vocal, conservative, anti-feminist women who work from "inside" the movement to discredit it. Candis Steenbergen (1999) explains that "accepting the insurgence of [dissident and anti-feminist] writings as an indicator of women's successful liberation and the impending death of feminism, popular discourse has perpetuated assumptions that Canada ... has entered a 'post-feminist' era" (10). These claims are harmful to young people and all feminists, and efforts to disrupt them will have a beneficial impact not only on the Miss G__ Project but also on the movement as a whole. The potential for this disruption requires that feminists record their own history. By making public the efforts of young activists to promote social change, I hope to join a tradition of feminists upsetting marginalizing negative stereotypes, acting as what feminist comedian Margaret Cho (2006) calls in true third wave fashion, "a bitch with a flashlight to guide us through this darkness" (xvi). By critiquing these efforts, I hope to maintain my place in a community of rigorous activists who believe in the importance of internal dialogue to strengthen the movement.

While I have used several Canadian resources in the writing of this book, in many cases it was necessary to rely on American work. This is a common problem in Canadian research on feminism, as Steenbergen (1999) points out, "the sixties' in Canada was distinctly different from the movement in the United States, but ... the mythology surrounding the decade has ... a distinctly American flavour. The same holds true for historical accounts of the women's movement" (1; see also Adams 1999, 17). Most writing about the third wave has been done in the U.S. and imported north for Canadian feminist consumption. This book aims to contribute to a much-needed body of knowledge about the work of specifically Canadian third wave feminists who are working within the social and political atmosphere of Canada, which is distinct from, although certainly influenced by, American forces. The Miss G__ Project, for example, is working within the context of Ontario's education system, which members believe does not "meet its own policy commitments to equity in education, respect for diversity, critical thinking, and the provision of a safe and secure [learning] environment" (Miss G__ Project 2007a). In 2004, Miss G__ began its lobbying efforts with only four steering committee members. Over the past several years, membership has expanded into the hundreds, with chapters of Miss G__ based out of universities and colleges in ten cities. Dedicated to anti-oppressive politics, the main goal of the Miss G__ Project has been to lobby for the institution of a women's studies course that would address the intersectionality of gender oppression, focusing on racism, sexism, classism, issues of sexuality and ability within a "white supremacist capitalist patriarch[al]" framework (hooks 1995). (In 2007, Miss G__ broadened its mandate so it would be a women's and gender studies course [see Miller 2007]. Pre-2007 references, therefore, are to women's studies, while post-2007 are to women's and gender studies.)

If the Miss G__ Project is not ultimately successful in achieving its goal of instituting a women's and gender studies course in Ontario's curriculum, I am concerned that it will be lost to history. Whether the project is successful or not, it is important that the story of Canadian feminism captures "the actual practices of actual people" (Smith qtd. in Naples 2003, 29) and not only the celebratory moments of large-scale goals that have been achieved. This is a major issue for the third wave, in which feminism is seen as having less to do with taking part in acts of direct lobbying than it does with a style of living. Audra Williams (2006) believes this to be partially caused by "feminist insecurity," which keeps third wave feminists from organizing the way other feminists have: "We don't join. We're not sure if we should and we can't seem to navigate the movement as it is" (19). She believes it is easier for young feminists to live feminist lives, making individual choices in accordance with their political beliefs, than it is for them to participate in feminist groups. This interrupts the possibility of capturing a real third wave feminist history, since the everyday acts of individual people are not generally considered newsworthy.

A view of history that only acknowledges those who "win" is

problematic for feminists, since so much of the success of feminism is in the creation and lived experience of the movement itself. A feminist approach to knowledge building as I have taken must recognize the essential importance of examining women's experience as it is lived daily (Hesse-Biber, Leavy & Yaiser 2002, 3), rather than celebrating only what has won public approval and been institutionalized in policy.

RESISTING LEGITIMIZATION: DIFFICULTIES IN STUDYING THE THIRD WAVE

We are products of all the contradictory definitions of and differences within feminism, beasts of such a hybrid kind that perhaps we need a new name altogether.
— Leslie Heywood and Jennifer Drake,
"Introduction," *Third Wave Agenda*

The third wave of feminism has been around for well over ten years, and despite a rich culture of activism, especially in the realm of art, music and literature, the movement has avoided coalescing into a large and easily definable social movement (Dicker & Peipmeier 2003, 29). Unfortunately, this has led to a widespread opinion that the movement is not "legitimate" in the way that other feminist "waves" have been. Young feminists, including members of Miss G__, who organize under the banner of a "third wave" have suffered from negative attention, partly because some feminists who consider themselves to be more serious believe that making advances in culture are not as important as making advances in more politically charged campaigns such as women's rights in medicine and politics.

Much writing within the third wave of feminism has taken the form of personal narrative (Jacob & Licona 2005, 197) and has been collected into anthologies or published independently. Many anthologies that host third wave writings, however, refuse to provide an analysis of how the personal stories fit into a larger political theory. This approach may be a useful way of taking the feminist debate out of the classroom and bringing it into the world (Orr 1997, 40). However, it contradicts the reality that most of the third wave feminist writings that have been published by mainstream presses come directly out of the ivory tower of academia, as many young feminists, including members of Miss G__, are becoming familiar with feminist principles through the women's studies classes they take as undergraduate students. This isn't to say that young non-university educated women are not working on feminist goals and campaigns on a daily basis, but rather that they may not be organizing under the banner "third wave" and may not have the theoretical or historical background to identify their place in the movement. Additionally, the writings of these non-university educated feminists are being left in their little-known zines or blogs, either by choice or by the problem of differential access to editors and publishers.

Jessica Valenti, a young American feminist and founder of the blog feministing.org, arguably the most popular feminist blog online today, has recently published a book entitled *Full Frontal Feminism: A Young Woman's Guide to Why Feminism Matters*. This book is a perfect example of current trends in third wave feminist publishing. The book is flashy and fashionable. It's funny. It's well written and engaging. Most importantly, it's completely accessible. It seamlessly melds theory and practice together, relating them through politics and Valenti's personal experiences. This form of praxis, which "draw[s] from our personal experience to inform and substantiate our theoretical contentions" (Jacob & Licona 2005, 198), is precisely what young feminists writing for a broad audience of young feminists are looking for. In her introduction, Valenti (2007) explains her approach:

> *Full Frontal Feminism* is not an exhaustive review of all things feminist. There's a lot of feminism out there — and you should check it all out. This book is just my take of it — my love letter to feminism and my invitation to my readers to embrace feminism for everything it gives to and does for women. (3)

Valenti's book is for any girl about town who wants to know more about the feminist movement, while being empty of potentially alienating feminist theory. However, Valenti herself holds a graduate

Branding Miss G___

degree in women's studies, enforcing the interesting reality that it is still middle-class, degree-holding women who are writing the feminist movement, despite the professed goal of taking politics out of the ivory tower. Of course, *Branding Miss G___* is no exception. And while I'm attempting to illustrate the work of actual feminists engaged in political lobbying, this group itself is made up of well-educated, middle-class women who also face this paradox of wanting to bring feminism into the public sphere for increased accessibility to all students, even though they themselves have had special access to a women's studies education in a university setting.

The negative attention faced by the third wave of feminism has come from both within and outside the movement. Young feminists have frequently been criticized for being apolitical and self-centred, partially in response to some young women's treatment of feminism as a "free-for-all." Nomy Lamm (2001) makes the oft-quoted statement that "if there's one thing that feminism has taught me, it's that the revolution is going to be on my terms" (133). This superficial approach to feminism is part of a backlash to already existing backlash representations of the second wave as being repressive and restrictive. Dicker and Peipmeier (2003) explain that problematic "free-for-all" feminism "doesn't involve a set of core beliefs that one shares or goals that one works for, but instead involves claiming beliefs and ideas one day and discarding them the next, as they go in and out of fashion or as they become personally or intellectually difficult to sustain" (17). This is third wave feminism at its worst: lacking political and intellectual rigour, self-centred, and trivializing and undermining of second wave feminism. It is this lazy brand of faux-feminism that gives the frequently good work of the third wave a bad name. The Miss G___ Project has suffered from these negative connotations when it comes to obtaining support from more experienced feminists who have been working within the second wave model. While some experienced feminists have been generous with their time and advice to project members, others have immediately written the group off as frivolous, silly and arrogant because of their playful approach to feminist lobbying and alignment with third wave politics.

The majority of third wave feminism does not operate in this "me" vacuum. Engaging with feminism in a playful and fun way does not necessarily imply intellectual or political laziness. However, it is fair to say that believing the third wave to be the first group of feminists to do so requires a short-sighted and backlash-fuelled vision of the history of the movement. The idea that second wave feminists are stodgy, repressive or restrictive is a common theme in a great deal of third wave feminist literature, responding to negative portrayals of second wave feminism in popular media. Despite the proliferation of these stereotypes, they simply do not pan out over the history of the movement.

BRANDING AN IMAGE

Our image is a good marketing technique; we're a good face for the Project.
— Lara Shdorkoff

I consider myself a feminist, and I have been involved in the Miss G__ Project since it branched out from the steering committee in 2005. However, my work within the Project cannot be understood as blind acceptance and support of all of the approaches undertaken by the group, including its emphasis on branding a feminist image that is extremely feminine, heterosexual-seeming and apolitical. When I look at the initial postcard campaign, for example, I feel torn in my support. I think a vibrantly coloured card bearing the group's logo of the Miss G__ head and text that reflects supporters' own experiences inside the education system is an intelligent and effective campaign. However, the conscious act of allying oneself with this backlash understanding of young feminists as being apolitical, even if it's as part of a "Trojan horse" strategy, strikes me as being very problematic. How are young feminists supposed to refute these negative stereotypes if groups like this one reinforce them as part of their strategy? This excessive femininity is used in order to distance the group from negative connotations that all feminists are lesbians, a distancing that effectively says "Yes, we know that feminists are lesbians, and yes, we agree that this is distasteful. Don't worry; we're not at all like that." However, I know, because I am an insider, that Miss G__ members are for the most part anti-homophobic. This presents a huge problem to the consistency of the group's message. Part of its mandate is "to combat all forms of oppression in and through education, including sexism, homophobia, racism and classism" (Miss G__ Project 2007a). This simply cannot be done as long as the group uses lobbying strategies that acquiesce with sexist, homophobic, racist and classist stereotypes of women and feminists.

The Miss G__ Project frequently uses a liberal feminist approach when working with institutions in an attempt to make room for women's experiences, and while I believe that this is a noble goal in many ways, I do not consider myself to be a liberal feminist. Within the group there is also a conservative presence, which I admit I find problematic, since many of the goals of the project go directly against conservative politics. Unlike most project members, I come from a working-class background, and I have encountered some barriers to working with the Project in terms of time, money and access to transportation and travel I am expected to contribute as a member. As a lesbian, I have many concerns about the heterosexualization of the Project's image. As well, due to my experience as a certified teacher and my master's research into the history of Ontario's school system, I worry about the goal of the Project itself, as there is a possibility that "success" may result in the adoption of a depoliticized "women in history" course in high schools. While there is no question that women's history does have a place in the curriculum, I am concerned that the adoption of such a course would interrupt the possibility of a truly transformative feminist presence in schools. It is a common problem in feminist activism that "the process of institutionalization often means that we lose sight of the larger goals of radical social transformation" (Briskin 1991, 34). Nancy Naples (2003) points out that when social movements achieve wide acceptance and become institutionalized, they often lose the critical feminist or progressive intent they had initially held. Consider, for example, the transformation of "battered women" into "battered women syndrome" or the depoliticization of "sexual harassment" (89). These concerns are held by many of Miss G__'s members, and so I am not necessarily at odds with the Project. Many of our group meetings become hours-long discussions about how to best navigate these issues. However, it's important that my position with regards to the group's strategies be clear from the beginning.

I am also concerned that the heterosexualization and feminization of feminist activism in the Miss G__ Project's lobbying events is indicative of a "dutiful daughter" approach to women's studies, as is described by Adrienne Rich (1986) in her essay "Disobedience and Women's Studies." According to Rich, dutiful daughters are interested in reform, not transformation. It is my belief that a truly feminist approach to a women's studies curriculum should require transformation. I believe that any approach that settles merely for "reform" harms the possibility of schools being sites of real feminist consciousness-raising and action, because to be dutiful daughters means to "play by the rules," and the "rules" of the education game require an enforcement of the status quo.

Lastly, I am concerned with the neoliberal attitude of what the steering committee continuously refers to as "the marketing of the Project," which relates to the "amazing capacity of Western culture to absorb oppositional, counter-hegemonic movements" (Lather 1991, xx) by adopting and depoliticizing social movement behaviours within a capitalist framework. This commodification of protest is common in the third wave, where feminism appears to be a purchasable and fashionable commodity, and often articulated more through slogans on buttons and T-shirts than group foundation and feminist activism. Of course, the Miss G__ Project has been consciously branding an image hinging on the logo of the Miss G__ face, placed on T-shirts and buttons that are sold or distributed at lobbying events or used on promotional and fundraising materials. This brand of "feminism for sale" is popular in commercials, where the co-optation of feminist and other oppositional slogans becomes marketable advertising (see, for example, Wetter 2006, 15). Perhaps the most widely marketed feminist slogan is Laurel Thatcher Ulrich's "Well-behaved women seldom make history," which over the years has "[kept] company with anarchists, would-be-witches, political activists of many descriptions, and quite a few well-behaved women" (Thatcher Ulrich 2007, xiv). Unfortunately, many of the commercial uses of Ulrich's words have departed quite severely from a feminist politic. In her book *Well-Behaved Women Seldom Make History*, she discusses standing in line at a bookstore and seeing her name and that popular sentence "on a dusty blue magnet embellished with one leopard-print stiletto-heeled shoe above a smouldering cigarette in a long black holder" (xv). E.K. Garrison (2000) explains that "for more and more subcultures ... the ability to intertwine politics and style is a risky and necessary tactic in a cultural-historical period marked by the 'logic of late capitalism,' in which the commodification of resistance is a hegemonic strategy" (143; see also N. Klein 1997, 87). I believe that the "branding" of feminism should be avoided, but Miss G__ members consider branding to be a part of the "business" of their lobbying.

GENERATIONAL CONNECTIONS

Perhaps it is more appropriate to say it is a product of the First and Second waves; the media backlash; violence and other kinds of historical remnants, products and monsters.
— E.K. Garrison, "U.S. Feminism — Grrrl Style!"

In addition to self-defining as a third wave feminist group, the Miss G__ Project shares many characteristics with other third wave groups in its lobbying approach and its political and cultural philosophy. It should be made clear that despite their connection to third wave feminists, the Project's goal to institute a women's studies course in high schools is very deeply entrenched in the work of the second wave. The fact that the group defines itself as belonging to one wave of the women's movement while continuing work that began in another, raises some interesting questions about the nature and usefulness of this "wave" metaphor to describe generations of feminists.

When feminism is discussed in terms of chronological "waves," the first wave refers to the suffragists, the second wave to the period from the 1960s to the 1990s and the women's movement for gender equality, and the third to the present incarnation of feminists, beginning in the 1990s. These waves tend to be taken up generationally, with members of the first wave understood as grandmother figures to members of the second wave, and members of the third wave understood as the daughters of the second wave. Many feminists have pointed out the problematic nature of this rhetoric, which compartmentalizes feminism in ways that are "inflammatory and divisive" and that "work ... to mask real political differences — fundamental differences in our visions of feminism's tasks and accomplishments" (Hogeland 2001, 107). Efforts to distinguish politically between these generational waves lead to a "positioning against" a mother–daughter metaphor, creating opposition in terms of "rebellion," which "has functioned to position [feminists] within what could almost be characterized as a feminist 'family feud'" (Purvis 2004, 100, 106). This wave metaphor carries with it anxieties that interfere with the development of political affiliation and coalition that are vital to the realization of feminism's goals (94) and, despite or perhaps because of this fact, the term is widely used by both feminist and feminist detractors.

Lisa Jervis (2006), co-editor of popular feminist *Bitch* magazine, believes that we have passed the point where this metaphor is useful, and argues that "what was at first a handy-dandy way to refer to history's past, present and future potential with a single metaphor has become shorthand that invites intellectual laziness, an escape hatch from the hard work of distinguishing between core beliefs and a cultural moment" (14). I agree with Jervis that this metaphor has become obsolete when understood as referring to waves as distinct generations; however, due to its widespread popular and theoretical use, I appreciate attempts by postmodern theorists to create new understandings of feminist time as "non-linear, multidimensional and simultaneous" (Roof qtd. in Purvis 2004, 111), so that rather than "passing down the torch" of feminist activism with subsequent waves supplanting the ones before, these "torches" may be passed back and forth, in order that each flame should be strengthened. Second wave activist Robin Morgan (qtd. in Dicker & Peipmeier 2003) called for this kind of understanding when she advised third wavers to "get your own torch. I'm still using mine and we need all the light we can get" (21).

This new, more postmodern understanding can highlight ways in which the second and third waves, working together rather than in opposition, are combating similar forms of oppression, albeit from very different subject positions. Jervis argues that what all feminists desire is bell hooks' understanding of "gender justice" (see, for example, hooks 1994, 17). This understanding can highlight the multiplicity of both the oppressions we face and the methods we use to fight them. When we look at feminist time as simultaneous, from the vantage point of the third wave, we may understand that second wave feminists are not necessarily our mothers, reluctantly passing us an outmoded torch we may or may not want to carry, but rather that second and third wave feminists are activists working from different standpoints, with different levels of experience, with agendas for equality that reflect factors unique to different groups but complementary to the overall goal of gender justice. Each of these waves must then be permeable, allowing for activists to be fluid in their approaches and strategies, giving to and taking from one another that which is needed and available. The Miss G__ Project has benefited from this approach, gaining access to materials such as "The Women's Kit," a collection of resources collected by women who helped to develop a women's studies course in Ontario's schools in the 1980s. These resources became a precursor to "The Miss G__ Kit," a multimedia teacher's resource that is still in development. This give and take can include sharing energy, criticism, financial or emotional backing, or a number of other possibilities. In the case of Miss G__, the members' efficiency with technology has helped to bring resources and networking systems to a wider group of teachers through the Internet.

Differences between second and third wave branches of feminism can be understood in terms of both substance and style. Substance may refer to differences in political philosophy, while style may refer to differences in strategy. Third wavers Baumgardner and Richards (2000) embrace the generational metaphor, and write that "we're not doing feminism the same way that the seventies feminists did it; being liberated doesn't mean copying what came before, but finding one's own way — a way that is genuine to one's generation" (130). Third wave feminism responds directly to the late twentieth and early twenty-first centuries from which arises "a world of global capitalism and information technology, postmodernism and postcolonialism and environmental degradation" (Dicker & Peipmeier 2003, 10). Third wave feminists are "experts in cultural production and consumption" (Riordan 2001, 284), having grown up with access to photocopiers, computers, music and video recording devices, the rapid growth of the Internet and the ability to create cultural resistance easily and spread it widely. Cultural production and consumption is, in many ways, the ideal entry point to activism for young feminists today. This often appears as "play" to older, more experienced feminists, who may believe that this cultural production "doesn't always look activist enough" (Heywood & Drake 1997a, 4). While neither the first nor the second wave of feminism subscribed to a "politics of purity" (52) that separated politics and culture, the obsession with culture that typifies third wave feminism often seems to other activists like a stopping point rather than a starting point for feminist activism.

Third wave feminists are often understood as standing "against" the second wave, positioned in opposition to much of the feminist work that has preceded them (see, for example, Bailey 1997). This has come about mainly because "writers and theorists love oppositional categories — they make things so much easier to talk about" (Jervis 2006, 14). The master narrative of oppositional feminist groups works well in the press and is even more effective for feminism's detractors, who benefit from a public image of feminism as splintered and warring, whether or not this reflects the reality of the movement.

The continued work of experienced second wave feminists such as Rebecca Coulter and Judy Rebick with the Miss G__ Project demonstrates a desire for a "mediated feminist community" (Purvis 2004, 101), which requires a willingness to attempt to understand the differences among feminists in order to improve critique and practice. The fact that Miss G__ members and their feminist role models sometimes disagree over approaches to activism is not detrimental to the movement in and of itself. Jervis (2006) believes that these conflicts are essential to the growth of feminism, arguing that

> feminism has always thrived on and grown from internal discussions and disagreements. Our many different and often opposing perspectives are what is pushing us forward, honing our theories, refining our tactics, driving us toward a more thorough dismantling of the white supremacist capitalist patriarchy (to borrow another phrase from [bell] hooks). (17)

In many ways, the Miss G__ Project is building on the second wave theory and practice members learned in their women's studies classrooms. This actualization of "women's studies" theory is not uncommon in the third wave. As Purvis (2004) argues, third wave feminists "have effectively put their backgrounds in women's studies to work for politics" (100). However, some second wave feminists look on aspects of the third wave, such as its reluctance to work collectively and its propensity to equate issues like owning record labels to running abortion caravans (Williams 2006, 19), and wonder just how effectively this theory is being mobilized. Feminism's third wave is built on both the politics and practices of second wave feminism, which inform it historically, as well as the backlash which responded to it within a postmodern, neoliberalist world where culture rather than politics is taken to be the key area of resistance. This is not to say that third wave and other young feminists do not work to transform politics and institutions, as the Miss

G__ Project illustrates, but rather that the movement seems fuelled by and focused on culture to a large degree. Garrison (2000) suggests that to understand the third wave we must understand its "cultural geography," namely,

> the material, political, social, ideological and discursive landscapes that constitute the context, base, or environment of third wave feminism. Young women who come to feminist consciousness ... in the late twentieth century ... haven't gone through Second Wave feminism themselves. Rather, they experience and are affected by it in historicized, narrativized form ... The third wave can be defined by a different set of historical events and ideological movements, especially the ... backlash that emerged in response to the women's movement in the 1970s. (141–142)

For many women in the second wave, the moment of feminist realization changed the way they interacted with their families, their friends, their workplaces and the world. Whether they came to it in their teens or their adult lives, many second wave feminists can detail the process of "becoming feminist." Gloria Steinem (1995a) notes: "In my generation we came to feminism as adults. Our revelations came from listening to one another's very different lives, discovering shared themes, realizing we were neither crazy nor alone, and evolving theories as peers" (xiv). Differently, many third wave feminists describe themselves as drinking feminism in without realizing its presence. Canadian feminist and author Susan G. Cole (qtd. in Steenbergen 1999) argues that

> to many young women, the word "feminism" is not charged with a sense of newness and excitement the way it was twenty-five years ago. They don't experience feminist ideas as a fresh body of breakthrough cosmic concepts that reverberate wildly through their consciousness. They don't relate to feminist thought as something they need in the way we needed it twenty-five years ago. (105–106)

While sexism and inequality continue to be present in the lives of young girls, these are considered "feminism's unfinished business" (Findlen 2001, xiv). Baumgardner and Richards (2000) claim that

Branding Miss G___

"after thirty years of feminism, the world we inhabit barely resembles the world we were born into" (9). Some young people describe themselves as "movement babies," carted around to consciousness-raising groups and protests by their second wave mothers. The feminist poet Alix Olson (2006) describes her own upbringing with feminism in her poem "Womyn Before":

> i was still sucking my thumb/ the first time i sang "we shall overcome"/ it was a numb december night/ it was a small town fable/ my first corporate villain/ and my mother was the hero/ allen ginsberg tradition, howling "human rights for workers!"/ like june jordan or barbara smith/ sonia sanchez and adrienne rich/ like flannery o'conner, like ruth ellis/ angela davis and mary daly/ bell hooks and flo kennedy/ gertrude stein, dorothy allison/ my mother. (8-9)

Of course, not every young feminist was born into a household so steeped in feminist history. Nor are all parents of third wave feminists supporters of feminism. This became apparent to me during my interviews with Miss G___ members Rawal and Mohan, who discussed their parents' discomfort with the word "feminist" (see chapter 3). However, whether young feminists have feminist or anti-feminist parents, there is no question that the world inhabited by young people, and particularly young women, today owes a great deal to the "women's libbers" of the second wave.

GET[TING] SMART: INFORMING OUR CRITICISM

You may be from the generation that once warned "never trust anyone over thirty," but now you're not so sure you trust anyone under thirty. This isn't just ageism. It's because you got bashed both coming and going.
— Robin Morgan, "To Vintage Feminists"

It would be nice if you didn't believe most of what's been written about older feminists — or at least read between the lines — and balance that by reading the work of the women themselves.
— Robin Morgan, "To Younger Women"

INTRODUCTION: LAUNCHING THE BRAND·

The gratitude for the hard work of the second wave described by Baumgardner and Richards (2000) does not preclude what I would consider to be a healthy criticism for some aspects or forms of prior feminist activisms. It is vital to the growth of feminism that healthy discussion and debate take place both within and across feminist movements. However, it becomes problematic when they are based on misinformation, such as the backlash caricature of second wave feminists as hairy, strident, man-hating lesbians, or the one formed by modern liberal groups that the second wave is made up of white, middle-class homophobes, or the media's representation of third wave feminists as ungrateful dissenters who only care about their right to shop and do strip aerobics. While some of these images may be based on partial truths of some aspects of the movement, the danger is that they lead to an incomplete picture which is intended to manipulate, demean, trivialize and demonize feminists. A positive critique of goals and approaches must be based on a more solid understanding, and until activists across the feminist spectrum educate themselves enough to look past such caricatures, all argument will be mired in misrepresentation, misunderstanding and a failure to discuss, debate and act. Madelyn Detloff (1997) points out that

> a second wave feminist ... may believe that a third waver's criticism of the second wave (for its ethnocentrism, heterocentrism, utopianism and so on) is tantamount to saying "All your hard work is worthless." The accuracy of the specific criticism is beside the point in these exchanges, for the discussion rarely gets to the level of weighing and considering the potential constructiveness of a particular criticism ... instead the discussion often becomes mired in defensiveness, for it evokes notions of betrayal and betrayed. (86)

Many third wave feminists are aware of the gulf that stands between the waves. According to Baumgardner and Richards (2000), "up close, third wave language and tactics are often viewed with misunderstanding and contempt" (227). Dicker and Peipmeier (2003) attempt to clarify their relationship to the second wave:

> Typically, the third wave is thought of as a younger generation's

feminism, one that rejects traditional — or stereotypical — understandings of feminism and as such is antithetical to its supposed predecessor, the second wave. The feminism we claim, however, aligns itself with second wave strategies for recognizing and addressing structural inequalities. (5)

According to Heywood and Drake (1997), third wave feminism "contains elements of second wave critique of beauty culture, sexual abuse and power structures while also acknowledging and making use of the pleasure, danger and defining power of those structures" (11). Rebick and Roach (1996) discuss the pressures young women can face in self-defining as feminists, as well as forming and articulating their philosophies of feminism within a previously established framework, staffed with more experienced and confident feminists:

> There's a mutual mistrust and lack of respect that happens sometimes between older and younger women. In the women's movement, older women have said "Listen, young thing, I've been doing this for years," in a dismissive way. And in the popular culture, and the book world, young feminists who diss our elders are promoted and touted as cutting edge, even though their critiques do not advance feminist thought. (94)

Many third wave feminists believe a defining feature of the movement to be that it "operate[s] from the assumption that identity is multifaceted and layered" (Dicker & Peipmeier 2003, 10), building on the works of second wave activists such as Maria Lugones and Elizabeth Spleman (1983), bell hooks (1984) and Audre Lorde (1984) who have struggled to promote an understanding of the ways that women of colour experience multiple sites of oppression differently and simultaneously. Second wave feminist Barbara Findlen (2001) explains that "our experiences of sexism are far from uniform: they have always been affected by race, class, geographic location, disability, sexual and gender identity, religion and just plain luck" (xv). Some third wave feminists seem to believe that this layered approach to understanding gendered oppression is new. Seasoned feminists know that "women's issues" have always been diverse and interlocking, and while a focus on pluralism may be an important aspect of third wave feminism, it is certainly not a new mode of understanding of the complex lived experiences of women's lives. The Miss G__ Project understands these layers, gleaned from feminist theory inside their own women's studies courses. In "The Miss G__ Chapters Manual," a guide they put together to help with the organization and operation of new Miss G__ chapters, they write:

> While, as a movement for the equality of women, feminism focuses on gender, we know that women are also affected by multiple oppressions, including racism, classism, ableism, ageism, homophobia and heterosexism — oppressions which intersect and overlap in many ways and which are held up by institutions in our society. (4)

GIRL TALK: METHODOLOGY AND METHOD

Participation demands alignment.
— Annie Oakley, "Interviewing Women: A Contradiction in Terms"

My research is informed by Michelle Fine's (1998) understanding of the possibility for feminist researchers to position themselves self-consciously as "participatory activists" whose work seeks to "unearth, disrupt and transform existing institutional arrangements" (211). These activists take an approach where all researchers, activists, informants and audiences are engaged in research as critical participants to "critique what seems to be natural, spin images of what's possible and engage in questions of how to move from there" (220). This approach considers that knowledge is best gathered through participating in projects (227) like Miss G__, as well as through studying them. Within the participatory activist framework, neutrality is impossible as well as undesirable. The pretence of neutrality is therefore counterproductive. Participatory activist research can lead to a deeper understanding of the political strategies that individual groups choose and the process of politicization that they undertake (Naples 2003, 31).

This kind of insider research could be considered problematic because of the researcher's close proximity to the "subject" (to use positivist language) and the great possibility for bias in studying those to whom one is connected. Outsider research has been thought by positivists to provide a greater objectivity. However, just as feminist educators know that there is no such thing as value-neutral education, we are aware of the inherent value-laden-ness of research (Lather 1986, 257). While insider approaches require unique validity checks as well as different, and sometimes greater, accountability measures, many feminist researchers prize insider research, as it provides them with greater linguistic competence, better understandings of cultural beliefs and practices and the ability to blend in with research participants more easily (Naples 2003, 46). They may be trusted more by research participants and therefore be "let in" on areas of practice that are kept closed to outsider researchers. For this kind of insider research of "friend groups" (37), I follow Naples in adopting strong strategies of reflective research that acknowledge how relationships in the field blur what we consider "data" and take into consideration the contradictions and ethical dilemmas inherent in insider research (38).

Activist insider research is difficult to undertake, for as Devault (qtd. in Naples 2003) explains, "using research results effectively to promote change requires the pragmatic evaluative and strategic skills of activism, honed through more daily participation in front-line work than most researchers can manage" (30). As well, insider researchers have the unique constraint of always being accountable to the community being studied (48), once again because of proximity and the relationships that are forged through study. So while insider status may provide an interest and a "way in" to research for feminist activist researchers, it also provides an intensified accountability to the groups or people being studied and the responsibility to engage in social change projects. It also requires an "opening up" or democratization of the research process that becomes a collective activity (31). This does not allow the researcher to take the perspective of the "knowing party" or "one true voice" (32), which can lead to discomfort. The point of critical inquiry is to lean into this discomfort and use it to help facilitate greater reflection. For the purposes of this study, part of my reflection process was to continuously engage in dialogue with members of Miss G__, so that I was not "the knowing party" but rather one member of a self-critical activist organization.

My main concern is with what Nancy Naples refers to as "women's political praxis," which often begins with the standpoint that women's "political consciousness develops from the material reality of their lives" (Naples 1999, 34), and involves the way women work to transform their own social reality. I have chosen to examine the praxis of the Miss G__ Project by critiquing the role that a cultivated public image plays in their lobbying strategies, because I believe it raises interesting questions about the changing nature of Canadian feminism, choosing appropriate lobbying methods, and the particular challenges faced by feminist groups in the realm of changing educational policy.

I have looked deeply into the Miss G__ Project through a series of focus group interviews with members of the steering committee, allowing me to use "experience, as spoken" (Naples 2003, 8) to build an oral history of the Project. In 2006, I met with the Miss G__ steering committee three times for interviews. During the first interview, we discussed the Project's background. Questions revolved around the Project's formation, goals and challenges, organization and consistency. The second interview revolved more specifically around the role of image in lobbying, as well as other issues relating to political strategy. The third interview involved a deeper discussion of the ways the Project is taken up by others, particularly in government, media and other feminist groups. In early 2008 I met with members for a final interview, allowing us to recap the Project's work in the past two years. This interview became a time for reflection on the approaches that have been taken in the past.

Because Rawal, Ghabrial, Mohan and Shkordoff are public representatives of the Project and widely considered to be the "leaders" of Miss G__, it was impossible for me to offer them anonymity. It was very important for me that they have the opportunity to feel comfortable with their words before I used them publicly, ensuring validity and increasing the possibility for honest discussion. During Miss G__ meetings, I discussed my critiques and suggestions for improved practice with them, and in the same way that some of their suggestions worked their way into my discussions of the Project, some of my suggestions were taken as starting points for improving everyday practices within the group.

A BRIEF OVERVIEW OF *BRANDING MISS G__*

In chapter 1, I discuss the background of the Miss G__ Project, including an account of the group's inception, and discuss Miss G__'s major lobbying events in 2006, the "New Girls' Club Luncheon" and the Feminist Read-In, both of which took place in Toronto. The critical focus of this book is how the Miss G__ Project, as a specifically and self-defined third wave initiative, relates to the media. In order to capture this relationship, I set the context for young feminist groups working in the current Canadian social climate, discussing what sets them apart from and what brings them together with other current and previous feminist groups. Feminism has always experienced a tricky relationship with the mainstream media, and I illustrate this by discussing the key "media frames" used to delegitimize, marginalize and demonize feminist groups. I use these frames throughout the book to look at the media coverage Miss G__ has experienced.

Chapter 2 focuses on the relationship between image, gender performance and the third wave, especially with regards to "girlie feminism" and the cultivated public image of the Miss G__ Project. I also discuss backlash feminism as it relates to the misremembered history of the second wave, which casts second wave feminists as hairy, ugly and angry, and how that affects the "feminist image" of young women of the third wave. In terms of Miss G__'s image, I discuss "branding" in terms of the Project's logo, the T-shirt and an emphasis on consistency.

Chapter 3 looks at image as a form of communication. Using a light approach to semiotic theory, I discuss how dress and image of any given group are understood by the public, look at the strategic deployments of both feminism and femininity that groups like Miss G__ use to gain greater public appeal. Of course, this leads to questions about the consequences of "playing the game" and depoliticizing feminism to make it more palatable. Building on my analysis of the group's strategic deployment of feminism and femininity, chapter 4 takes a more in-depth look at Miss G__'s media coverage in the mainstream newspaper the *Toronto Star*, the alternative Toronto-based *NOW* magazine, and the feminist publications *Shameless* and *Herizons*.

Finally, in chapter 5, I discuss the differences between the feminist and mainstream media in order to analyze the appropriateness of an image and media approach that relies on good coverage in the mainstream media. This chapter gives suggestions for media strategies that could better reflect the group's intentions and lead to a more successful adoption of the Project's goals.

Chapter 1

LOBBYING LIKE LADIES

Women can network too, and croquet is so much more fun than golf!
— Sarah Ghabrial quoted by Louise Brown,
"Young Feminists on a Mission"

ON MARCH 29, 2006, MEMBERS OF THE MISS G__ PROJECT HELD an event at Queen's Park in Toronto, which they called "The New Girls' Club Luncheon." On the guest list were all of Ontario's female MPPs as well as famous and inspirational women with different backgrounds from across the province. They included then United Church Minister Cheri DiNovo, who performed the first legalized same-sex marriage in North America; Judy Rebick, second wave feminist and author of *Ten Thousand Roses: The Making of a Feminist Revolution*; student supporters from high schools across the province; Project members from various Miss G__ chapters; and members of the Canadian Auto Workers (CAW) and the Ontario Secondary Schools Teachers' Federation (OSSTF). Also present was education reporter Louise Brown from the *Toronto Star*, which was the first mainstream publication to run a story on the Project in 2005.

Brown was the only non-student reporter to cover this event, despite Miss G__ members sending out an advance press release. On the way to Queen's Park, a car full of Miss G__ members, myself included, drove past a CityTV van sitting in a parking lot. Stopped

Branding Miss G___

at a red light, we called out to the reporter, who was lounging in the sun beside the van. We invited him to attend the luncheon, which was held just five minutes away from where he stood. He seemed initially interested, surprising us by asking a question about the nature of the event. Unfortunately, the question was, "Is there going to be a bikini contest?" This represented a truly disappointing beginning to an event we hoped to be charged with feminist social change. Instead of getting bogged down by that drive-by objectification, we cranked up the old-school Salt-N-Pepa we were listening to and drove on.

Beginning with a game of croquet on the lawn, the luncheon brought supporters and politicians together to share a light lunch sitting cross-legged on the floor of a banquet room inside Queen's Park. It ended with members attending the legislative assembly's question period, during which Miss G___ was introduced for the second time to the House by the then minister of women's issues Sandra Pupatello. (The Project's formal debut in the House was on December 8, 2005, when nineteen Project members attended and were introduced by Conservative MPP Elizabeth Witmer.) This was a great networking opportunity, as many members from chapters spread out across the province had never met one another, and many of us had never met our Canadian feminist role models. Just over half of Ontario's female MPPs attended this event, and several of them gave speeches of support, including Sandra Pupatello, who would soon become the next minister of education. Gerard Kennedy, education minister at the time, did not attend the event himself, but when questioned by reporters he also gave verbal support to the Project and recognized the importance of its goals.

The event was named in reference to the traditional "Old Boys' Club," from which women have long been excluded. According to members of Miss G___:

> The Old Boys' Club operates on a daily basis: in the guys' locker room, strip clubs, and on the golf-course — thereby keeping women out of science classes, the board room and the House of Representatives. We've got a lot of beefs with that most exclusive and elusive of clubs, but rather than "man-up" and try to bust into the club house, we think

we should be busting down the barriers instead. (The Miss G__ Project 2006b, n.p.)

As well, the New Girls' Club was a nod to the "Old Girls," "the many brave and remarkable women who came before us, the reason we've all made it so far" (ibid.).

While all members of Miss G__ were instructed to dress appropriately for the luncheon in "business casual attire" that reflected a level of respect and decorum appropriate to the venue, the four members of the steering committee decided to wear vintage-style dresses with blue stockings, in reference to the eighteenth-century women's educational group of the same name. The term "bluestocking" has been wielded against intellectual or literary women for centuries, which is exactly the kind of negativity Miss G__ likes to reappropriate in their lobbying style. The steering committee and some other members also wore sashes reading "Miss Educated" during their spirited croquet game, a spoof on the golfing tendencies of the Old Boys' Club.

When the *Toronto Star* reporter arrived, members were running around the park, chasing and whacking croquet balls about. In order to protect the Queen's Park lawns, members were not allowed to plant the hoops in the ground, so they improvised, using each other's legs to score points. This was a perfect photo opportunity. The photographer moved the four steering committee members together, their arms around each other in the middle. One member was placed on one side of them with a croquet ball and mallet. Nine or ten members on the other side acted as hoops, all in a row. By the time the photo was shot, one of the steering committee members had taken off her stockings and appeared barelegged. When the large, full-colour photo ran in the paper the next day, she was disappointed, explaining, "If I had known how good it looked, I probably would have kept them on. But the reality is that they were uncomfortable!" After this event, some members sat down to a celebratory dinner out. Eager and inspired by the success and high turnout of this lobbying action, Miss G__ members immediately began to plan their next one over veggie burgers and salad.

Branding Miss G___

PUTTING THEIR THREE CENTS IN: THE FEMINIST READ-IN

Meet me in the streets 06.06.06.
— T-shirts distributed to Read-In participants

In early June 2006, signs with the Miss G__ logo began to appear on telephone poles around Toronto. They read, "Feminist Read-In for the Miss G__ Project. 06.06.06. Bring Your Books. Bring Your Friends. Show the Government You Want Women's Studies in High Schools." This event was planned to be one part old-fashioned sit-in, one part music festival. It was advertised on feminist websites: "Imagine your typical sit-in, but without the force-feeding and free love ... It will be the fabulous, feminist, education-focused, all-ages, geek chic, refined but riotous, irreverent to the bone Woodstock of our times" (University of Windsor Action Girls 2006).

Due to the success of the luncheon and the proximity of the event to parliament, the Read-In was also held on the lawns of Queen's Park. Members of the media were invited again, this time with better success. In addition to the *Toronto Star*, reporters attended from *Shameless*, *Herizons* and *NOW* magazines. The event featured contributions from musicians Jill Barber, Karyn Ellis and Elena Juatco, and from the local band Carmen Elle and the Whoremoans; literary readings from poets Lillian Allen, Tanis Rideout and A.R. Rawlings, and from authors Emma Donaghue and Judy Rebick. Rebick, who read from *Ten Thousand Roses*, led the crowd in a chant for choice in the style of her 1970s second wave activism. MPPs Kathleen Wynne and Deb Matthews as well as newly elected minister of education Sandra Pupatello also attended and read works by or about women that inspired them.

The image cultivated by the Project for this event was decidedly more radical than previous events had been. Behind a small platform on which performers stood was a large banner reading "Put Your Three Cents In, 'Cuz History Owes You One," playing on a lyric by feminist musician, poet and activist Ani DiFranco.

Over the course of the day, some group members began writing on their bodies their favourite "slanderous" terms to describe unruly women. Rawal was photographed with "Brazen" scrawled across her arm in face paint, a technique used by riot grrls in the 1990s. Rawal explained to me in a 2006 interview that "some things we didn't plan, they just happened. Like for the Read-In, we started writing things on ourselves, and that was just in the moment. I was like 'Hey, I'm going to write brazen on my arm in face paint' and it was a great picture." Mary Celeste Kearney (1998) explains this riot grrl approach to reappropriation:

> Radically refuting the misogynist messages perpetuated by the fashion and beauty industries that encourage girls and women that we will never look "good enough," riot grrls often call attention to the objectification of female bodies in patriarchal society by marking their hands, arms, stomachs and faces with provocative political slogans as well as with words commonly used to denigrate women (e.g. "slut," "whore," "cunt"). (158)

Project members did attempt to challenge beauty culture in their image at the luncheon by wearing their "Miss Educated" sashes. By marking their bodies with challenging political slogans and traditionally insulting words, Miss G__ members more closely allied themselves with riot grrl politics than with "girlie" feminism as they had in their previous lobbying event. This was intended to be a fun approach to reappropriation, similar to their premeditated, campy appropriation of beauty industry accoutrements at the luncheon. However, this more spontaneous and direct challenge to feminine norms, in which the body is supposed to be a site of beauty and docility rather than of power, can be interpreted as a movement towards somewhat more radical politics. Unfortunately, for some conservative supporters, this was interpreted as a movement towards severely radical and queer politics, causing a small group of them to leave Miss G__.

While the Read-In was also considered successful by Project members, the mainstream articles that reported it were generally disappointing. The *Toronto Star*, which had previously given their

Branding Miss G___

stories about the Project a degree of prominence, running them alongside a large, full-colour photo, ran a one-column mention of the event, illustrated by a small and unclear photo of a member's back in a "This Is What a Feminist Looks Like" T-shirt. *NOW* magazine ran an article that was positive about the event, although generally dismissive of feminism and women's studies as "encouraging [and] inoffensive" (Whittall 2006). (I discuss in more detail the media responses to this and other Miss G__ events in chapter 4.)

WHO IS MISS G__?

> *Believing that woman can do what man can, for she held that faith, she strove with noble but ignorant bravery to compass man's intellectual attainment in a man's way, and died in the effort.*
>
> — Edward H. Clarke, *Sex in Education, or, A Fair Chance for the Girls*

The Miss G__ Project for Equity in Education was born in a dormitory room at the University of Western Ontario's (UWO) prestigious Huron College in 2004. It defines itself as a "group of concerned citizens working together to promote equity in education, to combat sexism and homophobia through education, and to encourage active citizenship" (The Miss G__ Project 2007a, n.p.). Sheetal Rawal and Sarah Ghabrial, then second-year students at UWO, conceptualized the Project as a lobbying endeavour with the mandate of promoting gender equity in Ontario's high schools through the creation and institution of a women's studies course that would be available in the third and fourth years of the curriculum.

The Miss G__ Project took its name from the historical Miss G__, whose story was made immortal in 1873 by prominent doctor Edward H. Clarke of the Harvard School of Medicine in his book *Sex in Education, or, a Fair Chance for the Girls*. The unnamed Miss G__ was depicted as a top student, "leading the male and female youth alike" in school at a time when women were only beginning to obtain higher education in the United States. Unfortunately, during her period of study, Miss G__ died. Clarke attributed her death to the popular "Conservation of Energy" theory, which suggested that, as a woman, "she was unable to make a good brain, that could stand the wear and tear of life, and a good reproductive system that should serve the race, at the same time that she was continuously spending her force in intellectual labour" (quoted in Miss G__ Project 2007b, n.p.). While this theory may seem ludicrous to us now, at the time it was used frequently to bar women from education "for their own good." Rawal and Ghabrial thought that this unnamed Miss G__ would be the perfect namesake for their group.

The relative absence of a woman-centred curriculum in high schools became evident to Rawal and Ghabrial after Rawal began to take women's studies courses at UWO. Inspired by the material in these classes, Rawal convinced Ghabrial to audit some of her lectures. They found that the theoretical background offered in these courses provided them with new lenses through which they could analyze and articulate their own life experiences, in and out of the classroom, which had been heavily influenced by gender. They found that, by using gender as an organizing principle, many of the troubling experiences of their lives could be categorized according to marginalization, exploitation and invisibility. They began to reflect on how much their perceptions of history were altered when the contributions and unique circumstances of women were brought to the forefront. Additionally, they were struck by their new awareness that many of the rights and privileges they enjoyed as citizens had not been "given" to women, but had been won by the tireless efforts of their feminist predecessors. Miss G__ members' work is based on the belief that an education in gender and sexuality studies gives students "the critical skills to recognize the impact of androcentrism, racism, classism and heterosexism on society [needs to occur] more broadly and at an earlier stage in our education, rather than waiting until university" (Bromley & Ahmad 2006, 68). As Ghabrial explained it, "We thought, 'Why don't you learn about feminism until university? Where has all of this information been ... High school is the site of a lot of gender oppression. Why is that still the case after so many years of women's movements and activism?" (quoted in Cohen 2006, n.p.)

Ghabrial and Rawal believed that their own experiences of high school — both inside and outside the legitimized curriculum and classroom — would have benefited greatly from the kinds of critical spaces a women's studies curriculum could open up. They also found that the kinds of issues they had been confronted by while in high school with regards to marginalization and invisibility were being similarly faced by their younger siblings, who were still in high school at the time (Wells 2005, n.p).

At the International Women's Day Breakfast on March 8, 2005, Ghabrial and Rawal made an impromptu presentation about Miss G__, and there met UWO media studies student Lara Shdorkoff. She decided to join the Project, and shortly after, Rawal's roommate and partner in idea-bouncing, Dilani Mohan, also came on board. Rawal, Ghabrial, Shdorkoff and Mohan became referred to as "the steering committee." Together, they developed a political platform that was drawn from the precedent-setting women's studies work and cultural capital of the second wave (Bromley & Ahmad 2006, 8). They also devised a media strategy that relied on the powerful and popular "girl group-esque" image of four attractive young women working for justice as part of their lobbying mandate.

The Miss G__ Project defines itself as a specifically third wave feminist lobbying initiative, and while there are no hard-and-fast rules to categorize feminist groups, in many ways this group fits the mould established by third wave grassroots organizations in the United States. Many of the goals and struggles of the third wave are extensions of and related to those of the second wave, including the goal of opening up spaces in school curriculum for the work and participation of women. The strategic use of a cultivated public image has long been used in feminist lobbying but holds particular importance in the third wave, which is sometimes criticized for placing too strong an emphasis on appearance and not enough emphasis on politics. An emphasis on appearances is certainly a strong aspect of the Miss G__ Project's political strategy. This book investigates the role image plays in the Project's lobbying strategies, taking into account how they connect to the strategies of the third wave, the tradition of the second wave, the mainstream and feminist media, the provincial government and the non-feminist public.

While acknowledging the problematic nature of drawing on a "wave" metaphor to discuss the changing nature of feminism and feminist lobbying, my discussion of the different approaches to activism taken by feminist groups with philosophical, cultural and generational differences seems doomed to rely in some ways on this metaphor that has captured the public imagination and infiltrated the literature. In order to discuss the theory behind the forms of activism chosen by self-proclaimed third wave feminist groups such as The Miss G__ Project, I am forced to discuss the perceived differences between the second and third wave. Simultaneously, I must explain my belief that this is a polarizing metaphor that allows for simple criticisms to be levelled about each group by the other and that can be used by the popular press to delegitimize the movement as a whole. Referring to the second or third wave of feminism as a monolithic group obfuscates the incredible diversity of the women's movement. Some feminists, especially within the so-called third wave, which has been heavily affected by postmodernism, may argue that there are as many feminist philosophies as there are feminists themselves. In fact, many perceived differences between the second and third waves are actually examples of differences in cultural geography, time-sensitive social reality, backlash-fuelled media portrayals and political positions more than actual conflicting foundational differences in philosophy.

A discussion of the supposed schism between the second and third wave is important to a group that defines itself as "third wave" and sees its lobbying as carrying a distinctly third wave personality; however, my main concern is to critique the effectiveness of using a cultivated public image in the lobbying strategies undertaken by The Miss G__ Project. The goal of this book is to evaluate and increase the possibility of using image as a political strategy in the most effective way for feminist lobbyists, whether they self-identify as belonging to a wave or not.

Branding Miss G__

At the outset, Miss G__'s hope was that their lobbying would succeed in bringing women's studies into the high school curriculum. The need for women's studies education in high schools seemed so clear to them, they had no idea that it might take years of constant lobbying to succeed in their goal. As Rawal explained to *Shameless* magazine, "We thought we'd go to the minister [of education], knock on the door and say, 'Hey, you should do this,' and they'd say 'Yeah, that's a good idea, right on!'" (Cohen 2006, n.p.). This seems so naive to the group now, since, after almost four years of planning and lobbying, the Project has not yet succeeded in its ultimate goal of instituting a course into the formal high school curriculum. However, the committee has been successful in spreading its message through press releases, media and information kits, seminars and word of mouth, and has set up Miss G__ "chapters" in eleven universities across Ontario. Each chapter is given a "Miss G__ Chapter Manual." It was put together in the summer of 2006 by a group of Miss G__ members, myself included, and contains a history of the Miss G__ Project; a feminist glossary; a reading, listening and viewing list; a Miss G__ phone tree; and other materials that could be useful for starting or running a chapter. It has suggestions on how to organize lobbying, fundraising and awareness events, and how to facilitate high school workshops.

A very important part of the Miss G__ Project's mandate is to do workshops that address issues of gender injustice in high schools. Miss G__ members approach and are approached by high schools to conduct workshops for groups of students, both co-educational and women-only. These interactive sessions focus on gender relations and sexuality issues in the school, covering topics such as the articulation of gender difference, the ways that gender affects relationships and individual lives and media representations of men and women. They are meant to provide a kind of consciousness-raising space, allowing the Project to spread the message that women's studies are a vital and missing part of the educational process, at the same time bringing issues of gender into the framework for discussion later in the classroom. These workshops are generally facilitated by two representatives, usually female members of the Project, as most working members of the Project are female. There are men who have joined Miss G__, and some of them have conducted workshops. When they have, they've reported that the students' reaction to a "male feminist" is one of surprise. On one occasion, Ghabrial facilitated a workshop with a male supporter from Miss G__. Ghabrial reported that when he came out to the class as a feminist, the students were surprised. The belief that men cannot be allied with the feminist movement is an example of misremembered history, as there have always been male supporters of the feminist movement. However, as the stereotype that feminism is just for women persists, the steering committee does believe it sends a useful message that feminism and women's studies can be for everyone when men conduct the workshops. Project members appreciate the opportunity to work with and spread information to high school students and their teachers at these workshops, and they think it is positive for high school students to see what actual feminists look like.

The "Miss G__ Chapter Manual" contains a section on "How to do a High School Workshop," which contains suggestions for a "dress code." Referred to as "Dress for Success," the Manual advises facilitators to

> wear a Miss G__ shirt if you have one. If not, wear another feminist activist shirt if you have one, but know your audience. Don't wear a pro-choice shirt at a Catholic school. You will not be asked back and it's rude to undermine a school's philosophy on their time. Try not to look like a teacher. Look like the cooler older sister/brother these kids never knew they always wanted. It will affect the way they react to you. (The Miss G__ Project 2006a, 23)

Miss G__ realizes the importance of impressing their audience. In addition to leaving an imprint on high school students, Ghabrial, Mohan, Shdorkoff and Rawal have also made an imprint on the public imagination.

Branding Miss G___

FEMINISM, FEMININITY AND DISRUPTING THE PUBLIC IMAGINATION

Let's run down the list: feminists are ugly, hairy-legged man-haters. Feminists are women who don't resemble doormats. Feminism is, as Pat Roberston infamously put it, "a socialist, anti-family political movement that encourages women to leave their husbands, kill their children, practice witchcraft, destroy capitalism and become lesbians."

— Lisa Jervis and Andi Zeisler, "The F Word"

Feminists have been painted in the mainstream media as ugly, hairy-legged, man-hating lesbians who seek to destroy the moral order and encourage fear and contempt in the minds of "normal people." This formulation is problematic for many reasons, including that it negatively equates a political position with a sexual identity, which is both ludicrous and homophobic. Unfortunately, these stereotypes feed one another, and it is often presumed by ignorant people that since all feminists are (supposedly) lesbians, all lesbians must (supposedly) be feminists. Because we live in a homophobic and patriarchal society, women who do not subscribe to a heteronormative traditional family life (that is, a family in which heterosexuality is assumed to be "normal" or necessary and where homosexuality is marginalized or maligned) are often demonized in the press as feminists, and feminists are branded as a force which upsets this supposedly "normal" and "desirable" lifestyle. According to Elizabeth Wilson (1985), "from the earliest days of contemporary feminism the mass media promoted a caricature of feminists — the bra burning 'women's libbers' who hated men but dressed just like them; a caricature virtually unchanged from [the] nineteenth century" (230).

In order to avoid these demonizing stereotypes, the Miss G__ Project and many other feminist initiatives have developed a public image that embraces femininity, casting themselves as "ladies," posing coyly in skirts, with full makeup, nice clothes, slim bodies and wide, white, straight-toothed smiles. Within the third wave, the playful approach to traditional norms of femininity is referred to as "girlie" (Baumgardner & Richards 2000, xvi). This movement towards a campy appropriation of femininity describes the approach of groups such as Miss G__ and is sometimes criticized as being "feminism lite" or "do-me feminism" by more conservative and radical feminists. Certainly, this approach raises many questions about the appropriateness of a feminist organization relying on stereotypical representations of femininity in order to promote social change. This is especially true for the Miss G__ Project, because the members incorporate anti-homophobic discourse in the curriculum of the course they promote, yet choose to lobby in a way that distances them from charges of feminist lesbianism. I question whether the playful adoption of femininity as a cultivated body aesthetic is a way to acquiesce to present-day social norms as unfortunate as homophobic anti-lesbianism and the desired creation and maintenance of "docile bodies," as coined by Michel Foucault and applied to feminism by Susan Bordo (1997) and Sandra Lee Bartky (1997). In this sense, "docility" refers to "those disciplinary practices that provide a body which in gesture and appearance is recognizably feminine" (Bartky 1997, 132). This theory builds on Foucault's idea of discipline through constant surveillance, but extends it to be understood in terms of "patriarchal domination" (132). The social importance of dress, especially as it relates to countercultural movements such as feminism, cannot be overlooked. Clothing plays an important role in "signifying practices [and] ways of generating meanings" (Barnard 2002, 38). It is important, therefore, to explore the semiotics of dress, giving special attention to the problematic aspects of the interpretation of messages communicated through dress. Malcolm Barnard (2002) points out that dress is

> the medium in which one person sends a message to another person. It is by means of the garment that one person intends to communicate their message to another person. The message ... is the sender's intention and it is this that is transmitted by the garment in the communication process. The message is also, of course, what is received by the receiver. The sorts of thing that are most important on this account of communication are the sender's intention, the efficiency of the transmission process and the effect on the receiver. (38)

Branding Miss G__

In this analysis, it is important to consider the importance of not just what message the wearer intends to send through a public image but also how that message is interpreted by a wider audience. As the Miss G__ Project considers its image to be a political strategy, the success of this image depends on how it is "taken up" in the public sphere and interpreted by the media.

THE (TROUBLESOME) ROLE OF MEDIA IN FEMINIST LOBBYING

The media is not fooling me.
— Ani DiFranco, "Self-Evident," *Verses*

In the developed West, the media play an important role in both shaping and reflecting public perceptions. In fact, "media definitions easily attain the status of objective and factual truth" (van Zoonen 1992, 456). Historically, feminist organizations have been concerned with media representations of women and especially how the media reflects and recasts feminist issues (Rhode 1995, 685). According to Judy Rebick and Kiki Roach (1996), "the media is supposed to reflect reality, but in fact it constructs reality" (37), and it does so in ways that are intended to benefit media owners rather than those it features on its broadcasts and in its pages.

From its inception, the Miss G__ Project members have been aware that the relationship between feminists and the mainstream media has always been difficult. They are also aware that the mainstream press is owned and controlled by patriarchal capitalist corporations with a vested interest in maintaining the status quo. Yet they also understand that good media coverage is important to the success of a citizen's lobby group. As part of the media's strategy, the members have worked hard to cultivate a public image that will draw media coverage, encourage positive reception by the public and earn support for the cause of women's studies from a wide variety of sources, including the non-feminist public.

FEMINISTS IN/AND THE MEDIA

The media is not in the business of doing public relations for social movements.
— Judy Rebick and Kiki Roach, *Politically Speaking*

The relationship of feminism to the media has traditionally been somewhat tenuous. Liesbet van Zoonen (1992) believes that feminism as a whole has not gained access to the media on its own terms, causing the movement to suffer from malicious coverage (453–454). While some feminist groups, such as the National Organization of Women (NOW) in the U.S., have been adept at working with the media, this may be attributed more to the professional skill set and cultural capital of members than to a supportive media. Over the years, many NOW board members have been trained lawyers, communications professionals or public relations specialists (Barker-Plummer 1995, 312) who have shared a similar class background with many of the journalists covering them. Unsurprisingly, the most positive coverage of the Miss G__ Project has come from journalists and writers who share similar class, educational and political backgrounds as Miss G__ members, and who have reported in feminist or left-leaning media such as *Shameless* and UWO's *The Huron Grapevine*. NOW also benefits from having interests which are not necessarily in opposition to the status quo, since it is a liberal feminist group that traditionally works *with* rather than *against* those in power. Of course, even NOW has had difficulty negotiating positive media coverage when it comes to controversial topics such as reproductive choice. For many feminists, relationships with the mainstream media have been oppositional, with the media covering social movements in "trivializing or marginalizing ways" (ibid., 309). Many feminists see the media as part of the patriarchal machine against which they are working.

There has not been a lot of specifically Canadian research on the relationship of feminists and the media, so much of the data we have to work with is American. This is problematic, as Canadian feminists have experienced a somewhat different relationship to the media than have their American counterparts. Miss G__ provides a great case study to explore this relationship in the Canadian context. Barbara M. Freeman (2001) believes that "women's issues generally received more equitable recognition in Canada than in the U.S." (239). However, in her discussion of the media and women's issues around the time of the Royal Commission on the Status of Women in the late 1960s, she also discusses the constraints Canadian feminists and campaigners for women's rights felt during that period to appear traditionally feminine, well-bred and polite, reporting that "female commissioners, and most of the women who appeared at Commission hearings, confined themselves to standard 'ladylike' behaviour" (95). Those who did not acquiesce to traditional forms of femininity were most commonly referred to as "feminists," and "aberrant or deviant" (81). She discusses women's efforts not to come off as "shrill" (87), and to be unthreatening to men, lest they be labelled as "feminist," or even, as "some kind of nut" (88). In these ways, Canadian feminists in the late 1960s were treated in ways that were influenced by American public images of feminists.

Freeman further reports that in Canada, in 2001, 28 percent of journalists in print and 37 percent of journalists in television were female, "a rough average of one woman to every two men, which is the reverse of the gender proportion in most journalism schools" (18). She goes on to report that a much smaller percentage of women held senior positions in either print or television news. These statistics are similar to, although not precisely the same, as trends in the U.S. It should be noted that Rebick and Roach (1996) believe that during the 1980s — at the same time that backlash representations of feminists in the American media were perhaps most rampant and powerful in discrediting the women's movement (see, for example, Faludi 1991) — feminist and left-leaning social action groups obtained a lot of positive media attention in Canada. Sadly, this abundance of positive coverage did not last, and the mid-1990s in Canada saw the reduction of feminist and left-leaning social issues in national newspapers (35). Although this illustrates that American and Canadian media patterns are not precisely the same, it may illustrate that media patterns tend to follow political patterns. However, I believe that both American and Canadian cultural forms are important to the representations that are given credence in the Canadian imagination, due to our oversaturation by American news and mythology.

Social movements such as feminism and the media have a mutually dependent relationship, where social movements need the media to help "mobilize members, to construct a viable public identity [and] to build a public policy agenda" (Barker-Plummer 1995, 307) and the media need social movements to provide the raw material for interesting news, especially photo opportunities. Yet this is not a "marriage of equals" (Huddy 1997, 184); rather, it is a lopsided arrangement with social movements more in need of — which translates into being more vulnerable to — media coverage than the reverse. Some have gone so far as to credit the media with being the life and death of social movements (van Zoonen 1992, 453). It can be considered that "the media not only act as our eyes and ears, they also help shape our thoughts by providing the information that tells us what we ought to think" (Wilson 2001, 94). Many individuals understand that, at best, the media provides versions of the truth influenced by a myriad of political- and ownership-related conditions. However, it remains true that media definitions easily attain the status of objective truth in the public imagination, giving media images a high degree of staying power (van Zoonen 1992, 456–457). As the majority of people will never meet the public figures they read about in the news, they must rely on the media to help them understand political issues. While it may not be true that the media act as a sinister "hypodermic needle," playing a propagandist role in the public consciousness, they do "perform an important affirmative function in reinforcing dominant norms and values to 'the public'" (Ross 2004, 61–62).

The Miss G__ Project is only one example of a feminist group which has been willing to compromise its message in order to gain positive media coverage. Many feminist and non-feminist activist groups have gained more positive media coverage by narrowing or concealing their demands so that they do not challenge the system (Huddy 1997, 185). Many feminists have had to become adept at this, as they are vulnerable to adverse media coverage, "because what gains attention for feminist issues often runs counter to what passes as appropriate feminine behaviour" (Rhode 1995, 693). Often times, the goals of feminism are supported by the majority of people, even when the feminist label is not. When the goals of an initiative differ from those of the mainstream, the press will often demonize, delegitimize and treat these groups as a threat to the social order (Ashley & Olson 1998, 263). As Rebick and Roach have pointed out, the mainstream media is a "corporate entity, and it takes corporate interests to heart" (37). This means the media have a vested interest in maintaining the status quo, and this support often comes through in what, how and when journalists are allowed to cover issues. Feminists who are media savvy and possess the "right kinds" of social and cultural capital, such as The Miss G__ Project, are aware of this. Their awareness allows them to tailor their appearance to "contain" their feminist intent in a media-friendly package. Members of Miss G__ achieve this palatability through the deployment of their cultivated image of "feminists can be heterosexual and sexy." Unfortunately, while this approach may help individual feminists to win media coverage, it does not seek to combat the underlying prejudices that cause the media to trivialize and marginalize feminist groups (Rhode 1995, 686) thus disrupting the possibility for widespread feminist media reform.

HOW THE MEDIA FRAMES THE NEWS

Providing familiar story patterns ... subtly [tells] readers how to interpret information.
— Carolyn Bronstein, "Representing the Third Wave"

A key way to understand how the media represent social movements is through "media framing." Media framing allows reporters to "bundle key concepts, stock phrases, and conventional images to reinforce common ways of presenting [stories]" (Norris 1997, 6). Reporters can use familiar images and sound bites to cue readers' understanding of current events. Frames can be thought of as "maps" that guide the public's interpretation of news articles (Bronstein 2005, 786). This is important because news sources do not have the time or space to explain the nuances of events, relying instead on this reserve memory of images to create stories (Erdman Farrell 1995, 642). By using principles of selection, exclusion, emphasis and presentation, the media are able to organize discourse in instantly recognizable ways (Ashley & Olson 1998, 264). In his groundbreaking 1980 work *The Whole World Is Watching: Media in the Making and Unmaking of the New Left*, Todd Gitlin discusses the ways that the commercial media use framing practices that are profit-driven and influenced by capitalist ideology to portray social movements in ways which are counterproductive to social change (Barker-Plummer 1995, 309). According to Ashley and Olson (1998),

> news media can frame a protest group in several ways: by ignoring it; burying the article in the back section; by the description given to the protestors; reporting the events rather than the group's goals and interests; trivializing the protest by making light of their dress, language, age, style or goals; or marginalizing viewpoints by attributing them to a social deviant. (264)

Feminists have suffered all of these frames in mainstream media, leading feminist researchers such as Rhode (1995), Bronstein (2005) and van Zoonen (1992) to use Gitlin's analysis to discuss the ways the framing practices impact on specifically feminist groups. It is important that social movement groups understand processes of media framing and learn to harness them because research indicates that by manipulating media frames, reporters can produce different attitudes towards the same issues, even within a single group of participants (Bronstein 2005, 786). Since the media does reflect and create reality, its framing of news holds a great deal of power for affecting the public's understanding, which produces direct consequences for social movements like feminism.

Branding Miss G̲

When the media covers feminist activism, they use several popular frames: marginalization, which is inadequate coverage of an issue; personalization and trivialization, which include a focus on women's physical appearance to divert attention from the message and issues of a particular movement; the polarization of feminism, which presents feminist groups as in opposition with one another; and deviancy, which casts feminism and feminists as being unusual and not relating to the lives of most women. In her discussion about how media framing relates to third wave feminists, Bronstein (2005) notes that the media have incorporated a "feminism lite" within which "third wave feminism is ... portrayed as a 'lite' option: third-wavers look great and have transformed the fiery ideological character of the second-wave into a friendly and approachable, but less substantive, brand of feminism" (794). This frame is tied to what British theorists Hilary Hinds and Jackie Stacey (2002) explain as "the new feminism" (153), which is polarized as "the *monstrous outsiders* of the 1960s and 1970s [against] the *incorporated Ms.* of the 1990s" (155; italics in original).

DISAPPEARING DISSIDENTS: THE MARGINALIZATION FRAME

The 1996 Women's March Against Poverty [which culminated in the largest women's protest in Canadian history] was an extraordinary event that took place over an entire month ... involving about 50,000 women from coast to coast. Yet the national media did not cover the march at all until it arrived in Toronto.

— Judy Rebick and Kiki Roach, *Politically Speaking*

The marginalization frame suppresses certain facts while including others in order to negatively portray an event or a group. By choosing what to report and what to ignore, the media can organize what laypeople consider to be important in the political world (Ashley & Olson 1998, 263). It should come as no surprise that women are under-represented in, on and behind the news (Rhode 1995, 686). Women journalists who manage to find work in the media have often been relegated to reporting on "women's issues" or writing for "women's interest" programs in various periodicals (ibid., 688; see also Freeman 2001, 13). The number of female journalists has steadily risen since the 1960s, thanks in part to the work of the women's movement and the socio-economic change this movement brought about (ibid., 687; see also Johnson 1995, 712); however, the gender imbalance continues to exist and may explain why issues that are considered to be of more interest to women receive less coverage and less effective coverage than issues that are considered important to men. Mainstream news ownership and editorship is male, and "hard news" readership is presumed to be male, which results in the privileging of men and male concerns (Ross 2004, 75) and the relegating of stories about women to "women's issues" areas.

Feminists have suffered inattention in the media in what has come to be understood as "Blackout as Social Control" (Rhode 1995, 690; see also Rebick & Roach 1996, 33). Historically, the women's movement achieved attention only if the issue at hand was the mythical "death of feminism" or if feminists provided an extremist tactic that could be exaggerated to deride feminists in the press. A good example of this is the supposed bra-burning at the 1968 Miss America Pageant in Atlantic City, New Jersey. While the bra-burning event was false reporting, it did provide a vivid image of feminists that many considered to be unflattering, yet many others lapped up. Bonnie J. Dow (2003) writes of the mixed feelings many feminists involved in the Miss America protest have about the mass media coverage the event gained, saying "the 1968 Miss America action is a source of both pride and regret: pride for the early visibility and membership it gained for the movement, regret for the unshakeable association of feminism with bra-burning that it fostered" (128). While this example is American in nature, it has permeated the Canadian public imagination of both feminists and non-feminists. Bromley and Ahmad (2006) argue that the bra-burning mythology

> characterize[s] feminists as radicals in the popular media, an image that lingers in feminist mythology ... the definition of women's ac-

tivism in these complex, intersectional [feminist] movements became constricted, demarcated and defined by the mainstream as a few outspoken radicals. (64)

Even though the event never happened, it became feminist mythology and some feminists embrace this myth wholeheartedly. For example, Canadian writer Lyn Crosbie begins the introduction to *Click: Becoming Feminists* (1997) with an epigraph about an urn her mother had on the family mantelpiece. The urn, engraved with the words "bra ashes," represented the belief that feminists in the 1960s made the palpable sound of coming to consciousness "every time they flicked open a lighter to burn a bra" (2–3).

BURNING BRAS AND TAKING NAMES: THE DEMONIZATION FRAME

If you are constantly told that the word [feminist] equates with hairy, ugly man haters, that it dooms you with never getting married, never having children, being unloved and neurotic, getting depressed and anxious, and being a selfish hysteric to boot, you are probably not going to run headlong to the office of the National Organization of Women with your membership fees in hand.
— Carole Rivers, *Slick Spins and Fractured Facts*

The demonization of feminists in the press has been a mainstay of media coverage. News reports frequently label feminists as "bra-burners, angries, radicals, libbers ... and militants" (Ashley & Olson 1998, 273). By creating a caricature of feminists as a frightening fringe group, the anti-feminist news media and those who use it can instantly delegitimize the efforts of feminists, even if those efforts are in the better interest of society. Freeman (2001) reports that in 1998, *Globe and Mail* reporter Terence Corcoran claimed that the Human Rights Tribunal's pay equity decision — which was based on the precept of "equal pay for work of equal value" and which favoured the lowest paid federal civil servants, most of whom were women — was a Marxist-influenced "radical feminist monster" (1–2). As well, in 2006, the *Briarpatch* editorial collective discussed an article in *MacLean's* magazine wherein Mark Steyn made several anti-feminist and anti-Islamic statements, concluding that "feminists and terrorists, hand-in-hand [are] working together to bring down Western civilization." They go on to emphasize that "[this was written and published] in Canada. We are not making this up" (2). This demonizing coverage has resulted in negative perceptions of feminists by the non-feminist public and has negatively influenced the willingness of equity-minded people to get involved in feminist activism because they might want to avoid the negative connotations that being a feminist carries.

"THIS JUST IN: SOME FEMINISTS ARE GOOD LOOKING": THE PERSONALIZATION FRAME

The media not only have a history of ignoring and misrepresenting us, but they also have an incessant need to soften our image — focusing on trivial issues of make-up and clothing, rather than on the political and economic issues for which we work.
— Megan Seely, *Fight Like a Girl*

As many feminists and feminist groups have worked to avoid the charges of extremism, stridency and lesbianism in the backlash press, many have planned their protests around a "lighter touch" (Rhode 1995, 696). Some feminist groups have opted to run their protests through bake sales, in order to remain "feminine" in the public eye, and attractive feminists doing "girlie" things have become popular media fodder. This can result in a media frame which, while less abrasive than demonization and marginalization, is no less problematic. The undue personalization of women in the media affects women inside and outside the women's movement. Many news accounts focus on women's appearances rather than their politics. This includes stories that focus on what women are wearing rather than on what they are doing. In press accounts that personalize women, the journalist often uses an appraising eye to gauge whether women live up to a feminine ideal. Rhode explains that "the focus on appearance leaves feminists in a long-standing double bind. Those who defy cultural standards of femininity are subject to ridicule, and their cause guilt by association ... But feminists who take pains to look attractive are equally vulnerable" (696). According to a study by Ashley and Olson (1998), an undue focus on appearance was the second most common manner of delegitimizing feminists in mainstream American news coverage of the 1960s and 1970s (268). The first was the use of non-speech quotation marks around pertinent terms such as "women's movement."

The personalization of issues is problematic because it diverts attention from the issues at stake. According to Jonathan Gray (2001), "protests are performed activities meant to grab the attention of an audience, to focus it on an issue of concern" (64), but when coverage unduly personalizes the key people involved in a movement or discusses the activities of the protest to the exclusion of the issues behind them, protests lose the ability to focus attention on the cause at hand.

(DON'T) BEWARE OF GIRLIE GIRLS: THE FEMINISM LITE FRAME

I'm just a girl, I'm just a girl in the world...
— No Doubt, "Just a Girl," *The Singles, 1992–2003*

The "feminism lite" frame combines characteristics of the personalization and demonization frames. It also draws on the polarization frame, which casts one group against another, playing each group as an individual and casting complex issues as "for vs. against," "left vs. right" or, more specifically to feminism, "second wave vs. third wave." The polarization frame creates personal conflicts that often times do not reflect schisms so much as create them. This frame pits representations of strident second wave feminists against the "new feminism," which is conventionally feminine in appearance and behaviour. The conventional femininity of the third wave supposedly makes it better and more attractive, but the frame also depicts the activities of young feminists as frivolous and juvenile (Bronstein 2005, 788).

In her survey, Bronstein (2005) found that the demonization frame was reserved almost solely for second wave feminists, portraying third wavers as a "welcome improvement" (790), with the positive portrayals of the third wave almost always arising in comparison with past feminisms. This demonization was often accomplished through personalization, which emphasized the personal style of feminists over their politics, especially second-wavers' "supposed penchant for hairy legs, flat shoes and mannish clothing" and the femininity and attractiveness of third-wavers (791).

This frame is ultimately hegemonic in function, as it promotes a view of the third wave as so superficial it could not possibly be threatening to the status quo (Bronstein 2005, 795). This frame articulates that second wavers are serious or authentic feminists and are also unattractive and threatening and that third-wavers are frivolous and unserious, but also attractive and approachable. Of course the logical interpretation here is that "real feminism" is not desirable, while non-threatening, self-absorbed "babe feminism" is. While the third wave may look like a lot of fun, it is unlikely to be taken seriously by the public at large, including government officials and those in power. It is also likely to attract the kinds of superficial support that are damaging to the movement, and it reduces the potential for alliance and coalition building between young feminists — even those who do not self-define as members of the third wave — and the second wave feminists they are unfairly pitted against.

*

These frames provide groups like Miss G__ with a great challenge in their efforts to obtain positive media coverage. The simultaneous knowledge that any coverage will likely trivialize their efforts while emphasizing their appearances and that coverage is necessary to lobbying success, put groups like Miss G__ in a curious double bind. Because members of the group will be first and foremost judged according to their appearances, if they wish for mainstream news coverage to benefit them, they must carefully structure their look to acquiesce with the expectations of the public and also to reflect their personal and political selves. For groups like Miss G__, these two

Branding Miss G___

may be at odds, forcing groups to choose one over the other, risking either the success of their endeavour or consistency with their politics. In chapter 2, I will discuss the way groups like Miss G___ take their appearance into the public world of the media, and how the media chooses to represent the images they are given.

Chapter 2

THE THIRD WAVE, FEMININITY AND PUBLIC PERFORMANCE

We wanted to put new faces on the feminist movement. We wanted to make it hot, sexy and newly revolutionary. No more women's symbol with a fist through the circle, no more recycled-looking mauve paper ... Feminism needed elective surgery — a face-lift, a remodelling — but it also needed an ideological expansion so it could be more pertinent to contemporary realities and attractive to younger feminists.

— Vivien Lubaton and Dawn Lundy Martin, *The Fire This Time*

THE INFLUENCE OF POSTMODERNISM HAS LEFT THIRD WAVE feminism in a kind of a joyful paradox. The activism of the third wave is characterized by multiplicity — in terms of both action and identity — and the messiness that can go along with it. Heywood and Drake (1997) believe that

> the lived messiness characteristic of the third-wave is what defines it: girls who want to be boys, boys who want to be girls, boys and girls who insist that they're both, whites who want to be black, blacks who want to or refuse to be white, people who are white and black, gay and straight, masculine and feminine, or who are finding ways to be and name none of the above,

Branding Miss G—

successful individuals longing for community and coalition, communities and coalitions longing for success, tensions between striving for individual success and subordinating the individual to the cause; identities formed within a relentlessly consumer-oriented culture but informed by a politics that has problems with consumption. (8)

This messiness allows third wave feminists the benefit of limitless possibility to play with feminism's history and the current political environment to make activism that represents who they think they are, who they want to be and what they think looks pretty. A lot of third wave practice relies on Judith Butler's theory of gender "performativity," which is often interpreted to mean that "gender may be a performance that can be manipulated and politically altered as it is performed" (Dicker & Peipmeier 2003, 16). Essentially, this means that gender is a learned set of behaviours that becomes second nature to us through constant repetition — including the way we speak or walk, our gestures and the manner and amount of space we take up; once we realize that gender is performed in this way, we're more able to play with these habits and self-consciously "perform gender" in ways that are subversive or in campy appropriation of social norms. Sara Mills (2003) explains performative gender as "almost like a set of clothes that one puts on" (n.p).

Performativity enables third wave activists to playfully incorporate gender as an identity that "reflects a postmodern focus on contradiction and duality … making it camp" (Klein 1997, 208). In many cases, this means taking femininity to the extreme, in a way that has caused much contention between second and third wave feminists. According to Chilla Bulbeck (2005), "patriarchy trivializes femininity, the pre-feminist is trapped in femininity, the feminist rejects femininity. By contrast … postmodern feminists 'choose to do femininity' although the femininity they do is almost exclusively a performance of commodity femininity" (66). This is a very simplistic understanding of each movement's relationship with femininity, especially since it plays on backlash understandings that "legitimate" feminists "reject femininity," but it does represent an interesting shift. Bulbeck discusses how postmodern feminists do the things that pre-feminists did: wear pink, dress in frills, high heels, shave their legs, wax their eyebrows, knit, sew and cook meals for their husbands (always husbands), except that now with the knowledge of oppressive systems of power derived from second wave theory, they do these things "with an ironic distancing" (66). Baumgardner and Richards (2000) explain that by embracing femininity, women display "that [they] can handle the tools of patriarchy and don't need to be shielded from them" (141). Bulbeck (2005), a self-defined second wave feminist, finds this kind of relationship to the feminine suspect. However, she recognizes that the world inhabited by postmodern feminists is very different from the one in which she was raised; in today's world, the current state of "hegemonic neoliberal discourse" (73) makes inequality harder to discern.

Some third wave feminists discuss rescuing feminism from its outmoded appearance and approach to make it relevant to the lives of young feminists. Baumgardner and Richards (2000) define this new approach to femininity as "girlie," explaining that

> girlie culture is a rebellion against the false impression that since women don't want to be sexually exploited, they don't want to be sexual; against the necessity of brass-buttoned, red-suited seriousness to infiltrate a man's world; against the anachronistic belief that because women could be dehumanized by porn (and we include erotica in our definition), they must be; and the idea that girls and power don't mix. (137)

Within the third wave, feminists focus on a body politic that celebrates the strength of the female sexual body, while recognizing that there are structural forces, such as patriarchy and capitalism, applying power on them and constraining the way they are expected to behave in the world. Instead of rejecting beauty and sexuality, third wave feminists focus on asserting their sexual selves, not necessarily for the male gaze, but for themselves, allowing them to be both subject and object in their own sexual lives (Riordan 2001, 291–292). This is often interpreted as "sexiness and frivolity" (Dicker & Peipmeier 2003, 10) or as "'lipstick feminism': light on issues but heavy on vanity" (Baumgardner & Richards 2000, 255), but advocates of the girlie movements believe these criticisms don't do it justice. "Girlie" is intended to make feminism "fun and relevant and in the moment" (ibid., 161). Third wave feminists acknowledge that while sexual power may be indirect in nature, it is still a resource. Joan Morgan is quoted in *Manifesta* as suggesting that "there are times when winning requires a lighter touch. And sometimes a short skirt and a bat of the eye is not only easier, but infinitely more effective" (163). Naomi Klein (1997) goes further, "we reason that because our bodies are appropriated through looks or comments anyway, we might be better off at least profiting from it" (220).

I have mentioned that this form of "playing with" femininity is often considered problematic by second wave and more radical feminists. I would agree that approaches to living as a feminist that include, and even go so far as to rely on, performing gender in ways that conform to stereotypical male fantasies are problematic for a number of reasons. For one, the sexual politics of the third wave are supposed to be "freeing," as they allow women to date and sleep with men unrepentantly; however, they are incredibly heteronormative. While the third wave presents itself as a completely diverse and pluralistic inclusive movement, many third wave writings feature a kind of reactionary hyperheterosexuality. Although many third wave feminist blogs, zines and books give lip service to a queer audience, and many of the writers and activists who are featured believe very strongly in civil rights for the queer community, it is common for these writers to emphasize their own heterosexuality nearly in the same breath that they mention homosexuality. For example, the American website feministing.com, which is arguably the most popular third wave feminist blog online today (and a fantastic one at that), contains almost as many references to boyfriend as it does to George Bush. This blog is operated by Jessica Valenti, whose 2007 book *Full Frontal Feminism* suggests that, among other things, feminists have better sex and better relationships (with men) than do non-feminists. In an interview with *The Guardian* on April

17, 2007, she praised both her "feminist" boyfriend and the way her feminism has helped her find better boyfriends:

> I have better relationships [because of feminism]. In fact, as I was getting ready for the photo shoot for this article, the guy I'm dating (who also calls himself a feminist) tidied up for me so the photographer wouldn't see what a tip my apartment is at the weekends. Would my pre-feminist boyfriends have done that? I don't think so. (1)

Third wave feminism purports to rescue feminism from the heteronormativity of the second wave, and yet much of it appears to celebrate sexuality almost exclusively for straight people and the occasional "raunch culture" bisexual. These displays of femininity are deeply racialized and class based as well, as traditional notions of femininity are closely tied to notions of "whiteness," privilege and the control of wealth. It should be made clear that the four members of the Miss G__ steering committee are not "white." A more detailed discussion of the cultural background of the group follows; however, at this point I believe it is fair to say that, within this case study at least, class is a far greater predictor of one's ability to enact femininity than is race. "Doing femininity" either for work or play requires the deployment of capitalist resources, including vast quantities of time and money, which is often impossible — not to mention undesirable — for poor and working-class women, who still find themselves being the overworked and underpaid victims of white supremacist capitalist patriarchy (hooks 1995).

Despite the supposed pluralism and "messiness" of the third wave, "girlie" is a very exclusive and privilege-dependent form of daily activism. The question that must then be raised is, is this activism at all? If so, what does it act against, as it seems to be in accordance with the oppressive white supremacist capitalist patriarchal order? Some third wave feminists claim that they act against the rigidity and seriousness of the second wave, claiming new forms of feminism which attempt to "rescue" feminism from its supposedly unsexy second wave form. Of course, those with a deep understanding of feminist history know that the second wave was never rigid or monolithic. Those well versed in feminist theory would also understand that, in fact, when third wave feminists enact "girlie" femininity, they do so in response not to the "un-sexiness" of feminism but rather to the backlash representations of feminism that have been perpetuated by feminist detractors seeking to denigrate the movement. Inadvertently, through this "girlie" enactment of femininity, third wave feminists may work to the advantage of the patriarchal status quo rather than to the advantage of the oppressed.

SUFFER THE SECOND WAVE: THE FRUITS OF BACKLASH

Tell him the girls had a lot to talk about tonight. Tell him we're changing the world and it's going to take some time. Tell him it's no easy task creating equality for women.
— Ilene Chaiken, "Labia Majora," Episode 1, Season 3, *The L Word*

The second wave has suffered greatly from a backlash movement that took place for the most part in the 1980s and 1990s and that can be credited for many of the negative stereotypes surrounding feminists, especially the idea that there is "one way" to be "appropriately" feminist, and that this way is by being hairy legged and unattractive. This includes the idea that all second wave feminists reject femininity, believing it to be a mode of social control. While a much-needed critique of beauty culture was and is a major feature of the second wave movement, this is not a critique that requires that feminists embrace a homogenized, desexualized identity. Rather, these critiques sought to free women from a femininity that constrained them and that was seen as compulsory. The second wave saw theorists mobilizing brilliant critiques of beauty culture. Susan Bordo (1997) used Michel Foucault's concept of "docile bodies" to discuss the ways women are regulated through diet, makeup and dress, through "table manners and toilet habits, through seemingly trivial routines, rules and practices" (91). To Bordo, the expectation that women will chase the ever-changing requirements of femininity rather than working politically or creatively is crippling both physically — reducing the possibility for public participation — and emotionally, as women can never be successful in meeting these requirements.

Through the pursuit of an ever-changing, homogenizing, elusive ideal of femininity — a pursuit without terminus, requiring that women constantly attend to minute and often whimsical changes in fashion — female bodies become docile bodies — bodies whose forces and energies are habituated for external regulation, subjection, transformation, "improvement." (ibid., 91)

This criticism is often interpreted as anti-beauty, when in fact it is intended to see the body as a site of daily struggle against the normalizing and homogenizing work of the patriarchy. Bordo believes that "we must work to keep our daily practices in the service of resistance to gender domination" (105). This requires skepticism towards the images and expectations of women that abound in the mainstream culture. Many second wave feminists are also accused of desiring a homogenization of feminist bodies; however, homogenization requires a lack of the kind of skepticism that Bordo suggests in opposition to embodied gender domination.

Rather than requiring a homogenized feminist non-beauty culture, critiques such as Bordo's are meant to free women from all forms of compulsory and constraining identities, allowing women the freedom to be active agents in the world instead of merely decorating it. Many second wave feminists have also critiqued the sexual nature of many forms of power traditionally available to women. It has been discussed that, in the third wave, feminists are aware of their sexual power and willing to use it for the cause. However, these forms of power traditionally do not allow girls to have "direct access to economic or political power" (Riordan 2001, 291), which forces them to access power indirectly, through the male power with which they may align themselves if they are successful in attaining the right appearance. Gloria Steinem (1995a) points out that, in fact, "feminism has always stood for the right to bare, decorate, cover, enjoy, or do whatever we damn please with our bodies — and do so safely" (xvii). The misguided belief that second wave feminists are or were joyless or asexual is absolutely the product of backlash representations of the movement. In fact, "sexual equality, freedom and self expression were among the fundamental feminist goals of the 1960s and 1970s" (Steenbergen 1999, 20).

MISS G__ AND THE TROUBLE WITH GIRLIE

I've been a babe, and I've been a sister. Sister lasts longer.
— Anna Quindlen, quoted in Baumgardner and Richards, *Manifesta*

I have discussed the intensely troublesome political nature of the third wave girlie movement towards "girlie" enactments of femininity. The Miss G__ Project uses a "girlie" approach to lobbying, which presents some potentially problematic issues with regards to strategy as well. While girlie is intended to be fun and ironic, and to be read by outsiders as such, in the communication of a message there is both the intention of the speaker and the comprehension of the listener to be considered. Third wave feminists must concern themselves with ensuring their audiences are "in on the joke." As is mentioned in *Manifesta*, "the more you talk to second wave feminists about nail polish, the less they want to hear anything you're saying" (Baumgardner & Richards 2000, 139). The Miss G__ Project is conscious that their image only works if their audience "gets it."

In 2006, Miss G__ members attended the Annual General Meeting of the National Action Committee on the Status of Women (NAC), in Toronto, Ontario. The professed goal of the conference was to discuss the role of NAC in the future of the Canadian feminist movement. NAC presented a "three options" report, inviting members to vote on NAC's future. The first option was to keep NAC but revitalize it, the second to remove NAC but to start a new national feminist organization to replace it, and the third was to remove NAC entirely. Almost immediately the third option was taken off the table and, according to Miss G__ members in attendance, option two never came up for discussion. Initially, Miss G__ members were thrilled to be invited to a conference that seemed to hold such importance to feminism in Canada. Quickly though, they realized that their opinions were neither expected nor valued.

They felt as though they had only been invited to be the "token" young feminist initiative present. When it came time to vote, Miss G__ members abstained because they felt that only one option was being legitimately offered and that this option would not likely lead to any real change in an organization which, if it wanted to be constructive in the current climate, needed to make some very real alterations in policy and structure.

For some NAC members, Miss G__'s light-hearted appearance and playful incorporation of femininity, along with their fun-loving approach to enacting feminism, may have been unclear. "I think they [thought] we [were] just giggling," Rawal admitted. In other words, they were seen as being silly rather than serious. This cross of communication may have led to the group's perceptions that despite being invited, they were unwelcome at NAC and, more specifically, that they and other young feminists were being treated as, and accused of being, "a special interest group" rather than a legitimate feminist lobbying initiative. Of course, it should be clear that the fault in this situation was not solely Miss G__'s. I find it incredibly disheartening that a group with such a vibrant history might treat young feminists as a "special interest group" rather than as the future of the movement. I think it's fair to say that the interpretation of Miss G__ members, who have a strong organizational structure and who have seen considerable success in their lobbying and feminist work, was based on backlash misinformation and feminist short-sightedness.

It seems clear that one of the major problems of using cultural production and commodification as well as a playful incorporation of hyperfemininity to define a third wave feminist movement is that it can be incredibly exclusionary along class lines. Within the Miss G__ Project, class-based exclusion begins with the recruitment and organizing of chapters mainly through universities, which can be attended by those with some financial means. The steering committee members are ethnically diverse. Shdorkoff is a second-generation Canadian with a Macedonian and Ukrainian background. Rawal says "I like to consider myself ethnically ambiguous (laughs) ... both

Branding Miss G___

of my parents are from India so I'm brown-skinned." Ghabrial is a first-generation Egyptian-Canadian, and Mohan came to Canada as a refugee from Sri Lanka. Within the Project, despite the relative ethnic diversity of the steering committee, there is a severe lack of diversity along class lines. The fact that the Miss G__ Project's members tend to be economically advantaged is considered one of the main reasons they have experienced the level of success they have. As with many other grassroots organizations, the funding for Miss G__ has come out of the pockets of the members themselves, not to mention the hours of unpaid labour that have gone into development and lobbying. The time and money commitment required of the steering committee has been a strain in some ways, requiring that group members divert their personal funds — many earmarked for new clothes, textbooks or groceries — to the Project.

> *Rawal*: [We take] money from our pockets to pay for things too, less so now than before. I remember we were throwing hundreds of dollars into the Project. I had a shopping spree on clothing that I was going to do, but I couldn't because I put all of my money into Miss G__. It was really sad.
>
> (Laughing from other members)
>
> *Rawal*: No, it was! It's a sad story! Have you seen my clothes?
>
> *Mohan*: No, this was hot it was for the first few months of Miss G__, because it was just the four of us and we were putting T-shirts together and putting together the MPP packages and our mail-outs and all of that stuff was coming out of [our own pockets].
>
> *Rawal*: Even T-shirts, like iron-on shit.
>
> *Miller*: That must have been a really huge strain, because you're four university students as well.
>
> *Rawal*: And travel expenses and gas. I was lucky enough to have a teacher [hire] me to be a researcher with her, but the research had to do with the Miss G__ Project, so I got to get paid a little while doing Miss G__, but otherwise I would not have been able to have a part-time job or anything like that with this kind of work going on.

Unfortunately, this means that the possibilities of having a hand in this kind of activism are limited for working-class and poor students and individuals who aren't students. This class barrier to participation is considered by Project members to be the biggest challenge to the group's diversity; however, while they believe that diversifying their class base is important, they also attribute much of their success to the fact that most members are middle class and have both a privileged financial position and the advantage of the "right kind" of social and cultural capital. These forms of capital, discussed by French sociologist Pierre Bourdieu in his groundbreaking 1986 essay "The Forms of Capital," refer to systems of privilege that are passed down both economically and socially through families and which have a strong bearing on economic and social success. Social capital refers to a person's access to a network of people who can help them succeed by "knowing the right people." Cultural capital refers to social advantages with regards to forms of knowledge, skills, education, language and other attitudes and qualities, such as taste (47).

> *Rawal*: I think we're bourgeois feminists at the moment. I think [we have to be] in order to get things done at the level [of people] we're working with and having the meetings we're having. You go sit in Queen's Park and you see who you're working with, and it's white upper-class men for the most part.
>
> *Shdorkoff*: If we weren't from that class that we're from, with the privilege that we're from, I don't think this project would be where it is, because last summer [when a lot of key Miss G__ work was being done] none of us had to work [at paying jobs].
>
> *Rawal*: We need to go in there and we need to be talking their language.

This presents a paradox: while working-class and poor women are welcome to join the Project, and while their membership is seen as integral to its diversification, they would be unable to participate as fully as more economically privileged members because of time and financial constraints. The current members of Miss G__ are free to facilitate workshops and attend meetings and conferences in other cities on short notice, without worrying too much about travel expenses and work schedules. As well, because of differences in social and economic backgrounds, it may be more difficult for working-class and poor members to "go in" and "be talking [politicians'] language" in the same way as members from more privileged backgrounds. Working-class and poor members might lack experience in dealing with "white upper-class men" and may not feel as comfortable in direct lobbying circumstances, and they might not have the appropriate clothing for such meetings. On a personal note, as a member from a very working-class background, I had a lot of anxiety over some of the lobbying we did with the group. I had never met a politician before the "New Girls' Club Luncheon," and truly considered not attending because I wasn't sure how to act around MPPs and famous women activists. I was extremely anxious because I didn't know what to wear to such an event and was worried that I would either over or under dress. Growing up, my social networks involved people in the same social class as myself. So, while many other members of Miss G__ already had personal relationships with people in the ministry through their parents and their parents' friends, I was, at least initially, extremely uncomfortable in that situation. This is not universally true, and for example, many working-class union leaders feel very comfortable "talking the talk" to people in positions of power, but it is a reality that with economic circumstance comes a large degree of difference in both relationship and experience, which may put working-class activists at a disadvantage in lobbying events where "talking the talk" and appearing "ladylike" are considered strategically important.

MISTAKING IDENTITY POLITICS

One of our greatest contributions as third wavers can be to close the gap across ethnicities, to build upon the failures and successes of this movement, and to live a politics that is about, and represents, all women.
— Megan Seely, *Fight Like a Girl*

Within the third wave, there is seen to be a deliberate move away from essentializing gender as an organizing force and an emphasis on the fact that one's background — including race, class, sexuality, ability and gender — dictates the ways one experiences marginalization in the world, rendering each person's experience different. This is one reason that personal narrative is such as vital aspect of third wave writing. In the postmodern feminism of the twenty-first century, it is seen as impossible to say anything true about anyone except yourself. This is often understood as self-indulgence by second wave feminists, many of whom rallied to make change by using a strong and collective women's voice. JeeYeun Lee (1995), in an essay called "Beyond Bean Counting," writes on her difficulty with the word "women":

> These days, whenever someone says the word "women" to me, my mind goes blank. What "women"? What is this women thing you're talking about? Does this mean me? Does that mean my mother, my roommates, the white woman next door, the checkout clerk at the supermarket, my aunts in Korea, half the world's population? I ask people to specify and specify, until I can figure out exactly what they're talking about, and I try to apply the same standards to myself, to deny myself the slightest possibility of romanticization. Sisterhood may be global, but who is in that sisterhood? None of us can afford to assume anything about anybody else. This thing called "feminism" takes a great deal of hard work, and I think this is one of the primary hallmarks of young feminists' action today. (73)

Within this context, where many third wave feminists don't feel comfortable uniting under a label that other feminists have considered a universal banner, we see a kind of splintering off, with most feminist groups "hyphenating" their identities until the most specific possible point. Audra Williams (2006) fears that "we young feminists have postmoderned ourselves into paralysis" (19). On one hand, it's important to respect the identities of individual feminists, but on the other hand, it gets more and more difficult to organize as the commonalities between women become more and more fractured. JeeYeun Lee believes that the feminist movement has involved "an uneasy balancing act between the imperatives of outreach and inclusion on one hand and the risk of tokenism and further marginalization on the other" (Lee 1995, 67). The Miss G__ steering committee discussed the difficulty of maintaining diversity in one's organization without devolving into tokenism. In a meeting with a second wave feminist, they experienced a moment where "our third wave activism sort of met with their second wave thing," regarding tokenism and diversity.

> *Rawal*: Dilani, Sarah, myself and Lara were in this meeting [with a second wave feminist] and she said, "You know what you're going to want to do, you're going to want to get—"
> *Shdorkoff*: "— a woman of colour."
> *Rawal*: Yeah, a more diverse look for your group. And she was talking about visible minority-ness, so she looked at the four of us as the face of this project and she said, "You know, you might want to diversify." Well, I asked her how you do that without becoming tokenistic, and she said, "No, it's just about being smart."
> *Shdorkoff*: I didn't like that at all.
> *Mohan*: I found it hugely offensive. Maybe, especially because when an institution takes up the issue of racism as it stands alone, it completely alienates anyone who identifies as anything else along with a sort of racial classification.
> *Shdorkoff*: I think it's the difference between a second wave and third wave feminism, because we never looked around. I think that for the third wave it's intrinsic, that it's not just about white middle-class women. It's a natural thing to say.
> *Rawal*: And it's interesting that she never talked about class, you know, because we're all privileged and we all went to university.

At the time, Miss G__ members believed they needed to become a more diverse project, but ethnicity is not seen as being their problem, as the members are from very diverse backgrounds. They thought that the emphasis on diversity promoted by the second wave feminist was only concerned with the physical appearance of race, and that it was dangerously ethnically marginalizing.

THE THIRD WAVE: FEMININITY AND PUBLIC PERFORMANCE·

Several members of Miss G__ are in fact visible minorities; however, their diversity wasn't considered "diverse enough" because no one on the steering committee was African Canadian, and none of the members appeared South Asian "enough." The steering committee believed that this approach to diversity "seemed like this really different understanding of difference from [their own] understanding of difference, or [their] approach to organizing and identity," which they believed corresponded to the difference in modes of approaching identity across the waves.

Many third wave feminists have clearly bought into the belief that the second wave of feminism was ethnically and sexually homogenous. This is paradoxical, since so much of the diversity theory of the third wave can be attributed to the work of women-of-colour feminists working from the late 1960s to the early 1980s. Some young feminists are aware of the strong body of second wave writings by women of colour. Rebecca Hurdis (2002) writes, "I stumbled upon *This Bridge Called My Back: Writings by Radical Women of Color* [originally published in 1981] ... it was as if I had found the pot of gold at the end of the feminist rainbow" (284–285). The idea that second wave feminists were all white, all straight and all middle class is a popular belief that was spread widely by the mainstream media, strangely at the same time that the same media portrayed second wavers as all being lesbians and in bed (quite literally) with members of other 1960s social justice groups like the Civil Rights movement. According to Ghabrial, "When you say that second wave feminism was white, liberal, middle class and straight, you make invisible the history of women in the second wave who weren't that thing." Rawal chimes in, "And that's exactly the opposite of what we're trying to do here."

It is additionally paradoxical that in the third wave, many feminists see themselves as disrupting the supposed homogeneity of the second wave, because race and ethnicity did not seem to play a strong role in the way members of the Miss G__ Project understood their relationship to feminism, even though their cultural backgrounds are a very important aspect of their personal lives and family relationships. As Rawal says above, "You go sit in Queen's Park and you see who you're working with, and it's white upper-class men for the most part ... we need to go in there and be talking their language." While race could be a large factor in an activist's ability to go in and "speak the language" of a white upper-class male, for members of the steering committee, the ability to use their financial and middle-class social resources seemed to override any potential difficulties.

POSTERS OF A "GIRL":
THE CULTIVATED PUBLIC IMAGE OF MISS G__

Hey, if you can't wear what you like, who wants to be in your revolution?
— Alex Kates Shulman

The Miss G__ Project acts in the belief that image is a crucial aspect of their political strategy at all levels of activism. Image is viewed as a valuable tool for recruiting, conducting workshops, gaining media attention, lobbying and holding meetings with government officials and other possible supporters. The image put forth by the Project encompasses more than their clothes and includes language, planned events and deportment. The Project's members see their personal and collective image as easily manipulated, embracing a very third wave approach to gendered behaviour as performance. As performers, they discuss the possibility of altering how one appears and expresses oneself to the audience one hopes to hook.

From the beginning, this project has been engaged with image as much as it has with a more traditional understanding of politics. Playing with image has been a way for the group's members to have fun while working towards the cause, as is popular within the third wave. Following Emma Goldman's legendary requirement that her revolution have dancing, the Miss G__ Project requires that their kind of political engagement works with their personalities and style. When asked to describe their image, the steering committee explained,

> *Shdorkoff:* We're pretty easy on the eyes, you know, like we're kind of pretty, we're easy to look at ...

THE THIRD WAVE: FEMININITY AND PUBLIC PERFORMANCE ·

Rawal: [Our feminist professor] did say something like, you know, "You girls go in there with your cute purses," and Lara was the only one in the group with a cute purse at that point ...
Mohan: I think the image is that we're young, we're having fun with it.
Shdorkoff: It's high energy.
Mohan: And we do what we want, you know, like we have our own look and I guess when it all comes together, it's energetic and trendy.

This specific image relates strongly to the third wave tendency to embrace the feminine through the appropriation of "girlie" as a method of cultural protest. At the beginning of the Project, the steering committee was not very critical of the image they were putting forth, nor did they feel that they were in control of it in the media. More recently, they have come to see themselves as very much in control of their image, and they see it as being an effective aspect of their political strategy. When discussing the strategic aspects of their image, the steering committee believes "it would be interesting to see how much attention we would get if we weren't this kind of ideal, like if we wore track pants or were all very dyke looking." This demonstrates a problematic and narrow notion of what constitutes femininity, but it also demonstrates a key feature of the way patriarchal assumptions about "what makes a woman" have infiltrated the activism of Miss G__. After years of political lobbying, preparing government proposals and working locally to achieve their goals and promote equity in education, Miss G__ group members still believe that much of their strength lies in their appearance, rather than in the intelligence and strategy of their work.

The project plays very much with the contradiction of performing femininity while at once being critical of the requirements of femininity. Shdorkoff explains, "We look very feminine, yeah, and I think that the point of our group is to deconstruct and problematize those things but then at the same time we're upholding them."

Branding Miss G___

They see their feminine appearance as being "more hyperfeminine ... which creates a space for deconstruction." I will take this as an opportunity to analyze "this space for deconstruction" in order to determine whether or not this hyperfemininity is an effective strategy. In order to do so I will discuss some aspects of the Project's image, such as consistency, "branding" with a logo and T-shirts, and the heterosexualization of third wave feminist lobbying.

"COVER GIRL" ACTIVISM: A CONSISTENT IMAGE

Like a Madonna-esque consistent but evolving image.
— Lara Shdorkoff

Third wave feminism operates in a neoliberal context where the influence of globalization and capitalism lead to an "everything for sale" mentality, resulting in the "branding" even of social movements (see, for example Garrison 2000; N. Klein 1999). A good example of this can be found in the environmental organizations that are marketing everything from T-shirts to coffee cups to promote global warming awareness in an effort to brand their organization as a leader in the movement. Miss G__ members have clearly been affected by this trend, as evidenced by their tendency to refer to the promotional efforts as project "marketing" and to the identification of their work as "business." Part of their interest in presenting a consistent image relies on this rhetoric.

> *Shdorkoff:* Yeah, it's understandable and people understand it, they like it. It was never meant to be that way but it just works, and it seems like a good marketing technique, and I mean, whatever, if you want to think it's just like the four of us ... To make it clear, we've never said it's going to be just the four of us, it was never that, but I think it just works with the media, and you do what it takes, right?
>
> *Mohan:* Yeah, like spokespeople, you need the face.
>
> *Rawal:* And I think sometimes, the public latches on to a face.

The steering committee believes that a consistent image is important because "people need to connect to something when they're thinking about the Project." Especially in the early stages of organizing, it was important that the public would see repeated shots of the same attractive people, dressed similarly, creating instant recognition. Mohan explains,

> Especially in the early stages, if your image isn't consistent, people might get confused and, if there are too many different images out there, then there are too many different interpretations of what you're about, and those early images are what's going to stand out in people's minds, so you have to be careful.

Of course this emphasis on "sameness" of image is paradoxical to the group's prior claims that, in the third wave, diversity is intrinsic. Mohan articulates the group's concern with providing a "united front" representation of their politics through the appearance of group members, requiring that the physical appearance of each member must accord with that of the larger group. Because media coverage generally focuses on "the group" or "the event," rather than on "the message," it is up to members themselves to provide a visual representation of the group's politics. In service to the maintenance of a consistent image, the Project has developed a recognizable logo, which, by appearing on every communication the group sends out, including T-shirts and letterhead, ensures consistency, allowing group members and their communications to be instantly recognizable as belonging to the Project.

"FREE MISS G__!": THE LOGO

It's become this very powerful symbol, [and when you need to be motivated], you just look at her face.
— Lara Shdorkoff

The Miss G__ head logo is present on the Project's website, on all print materials, on T-shirts and buttons and on four extremely large Andy Warhol-esque posters they hang for promotional events. Designed by Ghabrial, the face of Miss G__ is an instantly recognizable symbol that represents the Project and accords with their wider

Branding Miss G__

image. Like many other aspects of the Project's politics, the logo was born of a late night, an interest in pop culture and a knack for the aesthetic. Rawal explains,

> We had to do a workshop at the Social Justice Now! Conference in London [Ontario], and what happened was it was the day before and we were like, "Maybe we want to make T-shirts, we should probably get the logo together," and we had been Google imaging the word "girl" and the word "woman" and getting all these weird pictures like "horse woman"... So that was in mind, and then another thing was, earlier in the year I was going to buy a "Free Winona" shirt, I was going to get it in January, do you remember? It was when she was arrested [for shoplifting] and there were these big block letters and they said "Free Winona" and then this cute little Winona Ryder face. So those were the first things in mind. So [Sarah] drew one. In the first picture that sort of looks like Miss G, her face was not smiling, and we were showing it to different professors and they were like "she looks abused," "she looks beaten," "she looks sad," and we looked at it and we did think that she looked pretty vulnerable, so we turned up her smile and made her eyebrows look a little fiercer, and it was a logo made in heaven. Also, sometimes when it comes up at conferences or whatever and people ask where we got the logo, we just say we wanted something that looked good on a T-shirt, and she does look good on a T-shirt.

The logo has been criticized by some for the supposed whiteness of the Miss G__ image, although the attempt was to make her look "ethnically ambiguous." To disrupt the interpretation that Miss G__ is white, the group makes a conscious effort never to print their materials on white paper and not to make T-shirts with white backgrounds.

Miss G__'s face was given chin-length hair with a side part and thick-rimmed glasses, so that Miss G__ would appear studious. Current trends have many third wave feminists donning shirts with similarly smart looking women on them and sayings such as "Reading Is Sexy," as a sexualized reappropriation of the girl-nerd stereotype that many find empowering. This trend ex-

THE THIRD WAVE: FEMININITY AND PUBLIC PERFORMANCE·

ists as a backlash to the popular idea that men don't like smart girls, and it's been very effective for the Project in terms of gaining recognition for the Project, creating a symbol people will rally around and articulating the Project's philosophy through an image. The Miss G__ face is symbolic of many aspects of the Project's goal of opening up women' spaces in curriculum and reflects their interest in historical feminism and feminist literary theory. It also symbolizes the actual experience of Miss G__, whose name has been somewhat lost to history, and who has been long used as a symbol by men to keep women out of learning institutions. The members have described the relation between the logo's appearance and their goals:

Shdorkoff: Well, half the face is covered, it's symbolic in the sense that we're missing, and we're still missing.

Rawal: It's also mysterious, as in "what has she got up her sleeve." Also, the glasses were an important part of the design for her, it was the idea of clearer vision for one thing, and we wanted her to be a bookish, nerdy sort of girl. Also, we had all been reading a lot of Dorothy Parker and we liked her saying, "Men seldom make passes at girls who wear glasses."

The Miss G__ face has become so meaningful to the steering committee that some of them have had it tattooed on their bodies; hidden, of course, from public view. Shdorkoff explains, "It's become this very powerful symbol, [and when you need to be motivated] you just look at her face."

THIS IS WHAT A FEMINIST DRESSES LIKE: THE T-SHIRT

Feminism isn't about equality: it's about reprieve.
    — As seen on an Ani DiFranco T-shirt

Oh, you're a feminist, that's so cute.
    — As seen on a T-shirt worn by a male student at UWO

From the beginning, the T-shirt has been an important part of maintaining a consistent and attractive image. It has allowed both members and supporters to represent the Project both within and outside events, thus becoming the default "uniform" that could be worn with jeans or under blazers, depending on the type of event. The T-shirts were specifically designed to look like cute rock shirts, which could be worn tight and be "read" as more stylish than athletic. Somewhat consciously designed to be consistent with the "girlie" style of the group, they accidentally fit into the group's overall image. The members specifically chose a tight T-shirt that highlights a feminine body and "shows a bit of your stomach." They accidentally made the T-shirts in bright, feminine colours, because "it was the summer season and that's what was available." Over the years, the steering committee moved away from constantly wearing the T-shirts, for reasons as practical and fashionable as they were strategic.

> *Mohan*: [The T-shirts were] like a uniform when it was just the four of us. At the start of the Project we would always wear [them], and then … we sat down and we were like, "Yeah, at some point we should probably …"
>
> *Shdorkoff*: … wash this.
>
> *Mohan*: No, somebody once said we should only wear it when we're doing our big meetings, instead of wearing it every time, because at that point we had handmade them. So for one, it was preservation of clothing, because you can't sweat in [the same shirt] all the time.
>
> *Rawal*: Mine still smells instantly when I put it on … and I feel like there was a point where the image of us in those T-shirts was kind of everywhere, even just in my face, and I felt sick of looking at it, and kind of weird being like "Here I am, Sheetal from The Miss G__ Project!"

Although the group has moved past wearing the T-shirts to every occasion, they continue to make and sell them and even give them to high-profile supporters, which is a good strategy for spreading awareness about the Project. Rawal explains, "We have friends who go to feminist events, and they'll wear their Miss G__ shirts instead of their 'This Is What a Feminist Looks Like' shirt, or their Ani DiFranco shirt or whatever, and you know, it's exciting."

STRAIGHT, BUT NOT NARROW: COMPULSORY HETEROSEXUALITY

We're all straight here, right?
— Jennifer Baumgardner, *Look Both Ways*

The third wave's engagement with sexual politics tends towards a celebration of overt and compulsory heterosexuality, which attempts to combat the backlash stereotype that all feminists are lesbians. This homophobic identification of feminism with lesbians interferes with some women's willingness to identify as part of the movement. According to Barbara Findlen (2001),

> Some young women do fear the feminist label, largely because of the stereotypes and distortions that still abound. If something or someone is appealing, fun or popular, it or she can't be feminist. Feminists are often assumed to be strident, man hating, unattractive — and lesbian. The idea that all feminists are lesbians is scary enough to keep some women, even those who are equality-minded, away. When a young woman decides to identify as a feminist — a person who believes in the full equality of women and men — she soon discovers at least two things: that women of all sexual identities are feminists, and that, even so, she will now be subject to the same stereotypes and dyke baiting that may once have scared her away. (xv)

It is this fear of "dyke baiting" that leads some third wavers to over identify as heterosexuals and embrace femininity as a strategy against the assumptions that they are lesbians and therefore sexually suspect. To fight the stereotype that all feminists are lesbians on an individual level through claims like "me and my boyfriend are both lesbians!" (see, for example, Valenti 2007) may be an effective strategy for some feminists to protect themselves from dyke-baiting locally, but lesbians and anti-homophobic feminists find this kind of behaviour to be extremely problematic. As Gina Dent (1995) argues,

> Feminists are routinely "accused" of being lesbians or man-haters (as if the two are synonymous). Straight feminists often scramble

Branding Miss G___

to defy this stereotype by proclaiming their unfailing love for men and their affinity for bikini waxes. Some subtly distance themselves from lesbians by wearing buttons that claim "straight but not narrow." This is bullshit to me. If being called a lesbian is an insult to me, then I am an insult to lesbians. Any feminist who fears being called lesbian, or who fears association with a movement demanding civil rights for gays, lesbians and bisexuals, is not worthy of being called a feminist. (17)

Within the third wave, the other patriarchy-serving approach to sexuality is that of "raunch culture" lesbianism, which involves women participating in homosexual acts or creating the appearance of being bisexual in order to stimulate male desires (see, for example, Levy 2005). The rise of "raunch" may be best charted alongside the increase in videos like *Girls Gone Wild*, which feature young, drunk and potentially "empowered" women who exchange nudity and sexual acts for baseball caps and male attention.

The Miss G__ Project has been referred to as a "lesbian recruiting organization" by a conservative critic, and while the steering committee members regard themselves as being non-homophobic and hold the disruption of homophobia within schools as a goal, they have worked hard to develop a staunchly heterosexual image as part of their political strategy. When I asked them if there was room for a "lesbian appearing" woman in the steering committee, they responded:

Shdorkoff: We were talking about how having one — the token lesbian — is acceptable but any more than that is not acceptable in the media.

Miller: One lesbian is allowed?

Shdorkoff: One or two, one visible lesbian.

Miller: One visible lesbian in the steering committee would be okay?

Shdorkoff: Yeah, one would be okay.

Rawal: The thing is about the lesbian aesthetic, you know, things like window dressing, [well] our project still needs to be able to reach a variety of people.

THE THIRD WAVE: FEMININITY AND PUBLIC PERFORMANCE ·

The Project members are aware that an over heterosexual appearance can be alienating to non-heterosexual supporters, and one noted that "we were worrying that we might be alienating people who are transgendered [for example], the image as it's presented so far, or women who are rocking the dyke aesthetic." However, throughout the interviews, they seemed concerned about not wanting to alienate the heterosexual majority by appearing as "a lobby group of lesbians." This concern may be grounded in criticism they have faced from conservative supporters, both from parents and one conservative chapter, who have threatened to discontinue support if certain kinds of lobbying that may be interpreted as queer continue. At one point, our conversation turned to Adrienne Rich's concept of the lesbian continuum and it became very important to Shdorkoff, who is the Project member most steeped in media theory, to ensure that the group distance itself from claims of "lesbian recruiting," lest they be taken out of context.

> *Shdorkoff:* Somebody is going to read this, and they're going to say, "Miss G__ Project, lesbian recruiting organization," that's what's going to happen!
>
> *Rawal:* And I'm going to go up there and say, "Well you know, if we're talking about sisterhood ..."
>
> *Shdorkoff:* Just for the record, the objective of this project is not lesbian recruiting, just for the record.
>
> *Rawal:* No, we're trying to get women's studies on the curriculum, to make it clear ... We're a feminist recruiting organization is what we are, and not all feminists are lesbians, and not all lesbians are feminists. No! They are! Because I just said they are! All feminists are lesbians in a Richian sense. (laughing)

Shdorkoff's concerns that interpretations of the group as a lesbian endeavour could hurt the group's public image can be attributed to either internalized homophobia or an awareness of homophobia in the public and the media. Whatever the basis of these concerns, I would concur with Dent's (1995) previously quoted assertion: "This is bullshit to me. If being called a lesbian is an insult to me, then I am an insult to lesbians" (17). It is problematic to push for a course that supposedly combats homophobia while subscribing to homophobic discourse when it comes to lobbying, and no articulated concerns about "lobby strategy" can change that.

"BABE-MAGNETS":
THE ROLE OF IMAGE IN RECRUITING

There's a popular feminist shirt these days that reads: THIS IS WHAT A FEMINIST LOOKS LIKE. Ashley Judd wore one ... Margaret Cho wore one ... I wear one too; I love this shirt. Because you never really do know what a feminist looks like.

— Jessica Valenti, *Full Frontal Feminism*

The Miss G__ Project is always trying to attract new members and supporters across the country, and their image plays an interesting and difficult role in this process. Initially, group members had approached potential supporters at different feminist events. Mohan explained that when people wear physical signifiers about feminism, they're more likely to be approached: "You can't assume the right fit just on the surface level ... I don't think I could ever just pick someone out ... unless I heard them talk about [feminism], but then if you saw someone wearing a 'This Is What a Feminist Looks Like' T-shirt, you'd be like, 'Hey, get on board.'"

A lot of activists choose to wear their politics on their sleeves in this way for this reason. T-shirts that say "This Is What a Feminist Looks Like" are extremely popular among women's studies students, male and female, and make it easier to do feminist networking within the school. Of course this strategy is not specific to either the third wave or feminism. Activists and other members of the counterculture have long embraced the use of buttons, patches, T-shirts and tattoos to signify membership in a movement.

Growth across the province relies somewhat on word of mouth between friend groups, but it can also be attributed to the Project's ability to present themselves as a group worth joining and their cause as one worth supporting. In the case of the Waterloo Chapter, students at the University of Waterloo saw coverage about the

THE THIRD WAVE: FEMININITY AND PUBLIC PERFORMANCE·

Miss G__ luncheon at Queen's Park in the *Toronto Star* and approached the committee through the reporter who wrote the piece. When posing for photos in the mainstream press such as the *Toronto Star*, the Project's members are aware that they walk a tightrope of not wanting to alienate the non-feminist public, attracting other feminists and feminist supporters and drawing the attention of the provincial government. At the same time, they want the media to continue wanting to feature them. This requires a very strategic use of image, which battles between selling out and alienating the mainstream non-feminist public. The Miss G__ Project, which consciously considers their recruiting as "project marketing," has faced charges of both selling out and alienating the public from within and outside the group, pointing to the reality that some aspects of either its image or image-based lobbying in general are problematic and inconsistent, leading to misunderstandings both within and outside the Project.

This fine line between selling out and alienating the public is a difficult one for any group. In order to find political success in this model, many groups such as the Miss G__ Project come to rely on a strategic deployment of either feminism or femininity, as will be discussed in the next chapter, "Packaging a (non)Feminist Image."

Chapter 3

PACKAGING A (NON)FEMINIST IMAGE

[Young women] claim feminist agency for themselves and each other by making use of a historically situated repertoire of cultural objects and images, codes and signs in self-consciously political ways.
— Edlie Garrison, "U.S. Feminism — Grrrl Style!"

ACCORDING TO MARGARET MAYNARD (2004), THE MEDIA IS INcreasingly obsessed with the image and dress style of politicians (58). Dress style comes to be seen by the media, and by extension the public, as "telling" something about a person or an organization's politics. This may be even more true when it comes to women, as the stereotypical understanding of women in the public sphere continues to be reminiscent of Berger's belief that "men act, women appear" (qtd. in Barnard 2002, 113; Maynard 2004, 58). Semiotic theory understands that all human communication uses "signs," meaning that something is always standing in for or representing something else (Barnard 2002, 81). This is true for spoken as well as visual communication, including but not limited to written expressions, body language and the language of dress and deportment (Entwistle 2000, 128). As body language and dress together construct a gendered appearance (ibid., 178; Barnard

2002, 116), women have frequently used fashion to interrogate and protest against cultural norms. History is also full of examples of non-feminist social dissidents using special forms of dress to express revolt as well (Wilson 1985, 12–13). Think, for example, about 1960s American war protestors dressing in military-issue fatigues. Using clothing to understand and create understanding in our daily lives and political struggles is effective because our impressions of people and events rely heavily on what we see and how sights are interpreted. Political actors work hard to cultivate a public image that corresponds to their goals and desires and that reflects the social groups to which one belongs, "knowing that people read significance into such cues as manner of dress, body position, gestures and facial expressions" (Barnard 2002, 52–53). For example, Jack Layton, federal NDP leader, frequently appears in photos in dress shirts with the sleeves rolled up to the elbows, the way a "working man" might. This makes him look more like the people whose votes he wants to attract.

Like many other third wave feminist groups, the Miss G__ Project uses a postmodern approach to subversion through appearance, taking up camp, masquerade and gender play in their activism. These types of feminist activist aren't new to feminism in the twenty-first century, and many of the specific manoeuvres adopted by the Miss G__ Project are insider "nods" to work done by feminists from all across the history of the movement. It could be considered that past feminisms have supplied the tools and postmodernism has supplied the mood in which current work by many young feminists who self-define as "third wave" do their activism. In postmodernism, parody, ironic quotation, pastiche and intertextuality become central aspects of activism. Linda Hutcheon (2002) refers to this as "rummaging through the image reserves of the past" (89) to create powerful and evocative political moments. In this postmodern "mood," the study of fashion and its meanings has become quite "fashionable." According to Jennifer Craik (qtd. in Gibson 2000), fashion is of interest to postmodernists because its "slipperiness, [its] ambivalence, polyvalence, semiotic smorgasbord and excess fits into a worldview of consumerism, pluralism and masquerade gone mad — the unfettered circulation of free-floating signs" (355). While this fantastical and carnivalesque appraisal of fashion celebrates some problematic aspects of its use as a site of resistance for feminists, such as the excessive unmindful consumption in which women are socialized to participate as part of what hooks (1995) commonly refers to as "white supremacist capitalist patriarchal society" (164), it points to the possibility for a semiotic understanding of feminism's use of fashion as a tool for political activism.

Because much of the work of feminism has involved fighting gender oppression, and understandings of gender are so closely related to the body and practices of dressing, dress is the perfect ground on which to stage a revolt. This has been evidenced in many ways, from the wearing of trousers in the 1920s and 1930s, to moves away from restrictive undergarments in the 1960s and 1970s, to the postmodern woman's whole-hearted embrace of restrictive bras and corsets, to the thong underwear of third wave feminism. These are some of the stereotypical ways that the relationship of feminism and dress has come to be understood. While these are simplistic understandings, based as much on a feminist mythology as on fact, it is true that dress and dress-related behaviours become visual representations of political aims, either in the public or the private domain (Parkins 2002, 3). This includes the Miss G__ Project's decision to wear blue stockings and "Miss Educated" sashes, as well as the more mundane possibility of wearing a political T-shirt to a rock concert. While these visual representations are extremely important in expressing one's political interests, they can be dangerous because they are susceptible to different interpretations (Crane 2000, 126).

The Miss G__ Project uses its image as a political instrument to influence its formal and informal political relationships (O'Neal 1999, 127). In order for this sort of lobbying to be successful, activists must effectively use signifiers, or physical signs, to influence an understanding of their work — that is, their public signifiers must shape the way their audiences think or perceive them (Barnard 2002, 81). There is no doubt of the possibility that the feminized and heterosexualized appearance of the group may alienate gender non-conformists and queer members of the community. At this point it becomes useful to discuss whether the Project's public image carries an appropriate or desired "connotation" — how are Miss G__'s images acted out and how are they understood by different people. Drawing on Barnard's (2002) points, people's understandings of the meaning of "signs" differs "depending on their cultural situation," such as their sex, age or class (84–86).

When looking at image as a form of communication, the "message" — in the case of the Miss G__ Project, a desired change in educational policy — is made up of the intention of the sender as well as the understanding of the receiver (Barnard 2002, 30). Unfortunately for people who use image as a part of their political message, this presents the possibility that the sender can tailor their dress to "connote" a certain thing but the receiver can understand something very different and uncomplimentary. If the desired message does not arrive, or arrives in a distorted manner, somewhere the process has failed (ibid., 28). This might be especially tricky for a feminist group like Miss G__ that relies on an exaggerated femininity alongside insider nods to the dress and activity of feminism's past. In order for the audience to fully grasp the meaning, for example, of the strategic image used for the "New Girls' Club Luncheon," where the steering committee wore vintage dresses, bluestockings and sashes emblazoned with "Miss Educated" while playing croquet on the lawns of Queen's Park, they would have to have a cultural understanding of the "Old Boys' Club," the historical — and specifically feminist historical — "bluestockings" group, and the 1968 pageant. It would also be helpful if they knew the music of American vocalist Lauryn Hill, whose 1998 album *The Miseducation of Lauryn Hill* inspired the sashes, or had an understanding that in Western culture women have traditionally been instructed to cultivate good looks rather than good brains. The most complete understandings would come to those who knew all of these references. In order to

PACKAGING A (NON)FEMINIST IMAGE ·

understand the supposed "novelty" of good-looking feminists (as was discussed by the *Toronto Star* article and photo from this event), the audience would have to believe that feminists are not traditionally good looking and, in order to be impressed by the strategic humour of the group, the audience would have to believe that feminists are humourless.

This points to the reality that image-based protest is understood in layers, where groups that have the most in common with the political actors will understand the most and groups with the least cultural similarities will understand the least. This presents a problem of which the group is absolutely aware, that this kind of lobbying is only effective insofar as people are able to comprehend the messages the images carry. It also raises troublesome questions about what is the most "correct" reading of any event, a distinction that puts pressure on the receiver to decode in the "right" way, when the onus should be on the sender to be responsible with the images he/she want the public to decode. This is a distinction articulated by Miss G__ members:

> *Shdorkoff:* I think that the campiness and the satirical aspect are important, but then it's important that if the viewer doesn't understand it, then there's a problem, like you can only be campy up to a certain point that you know people will get it, like if we're doing all this and we're posing all hyperfeminine, if people are seeing that and taking it — the problem is not so much with being campy, it's the way that people ...
>
> *Mohan:* [It's] the perception.
>
> *Shdorkoff:* So, it's not just what we're putting out there but whether people are getting it. I know that there's responsibility there for us to be only campy to a point where we know that people might get it.

When an "in-the-know" feminist with a university background, preferably in women's studies, sees the "New Girls' Club" photo in the *Toronto Star* — featuring members laughing as they play croquet together in neat and clean clothes, some wearing sashes and blue stockings — she will likely understand that the blue stockings

Branding Miss G___

worn by the steering committee points to the literate and creative nature of the project, that the sashes hearken to the feminist historical background discussed above and that the croquet mallets satirize the "Old Boys' Club" and the tendency to strike deals over golf. She might also connect the playing of croquet to "aristocratic women" who have nothing to do with their time but have lunch and play lawn games, which are generally associated with the upper class. Depending on their feminist and political background, they might also view the explicit femininity of the group as acquiescence to patriarchy, or they might view the group as frivolous, silly or humorous. This presents an interesting reality — that the group most likely to pick up on most of the connotative meanings of this photo could either be interested in or turned off by the "girlie" approach.

According to group members, university or college students of a similar age, or high school students who share a similar cultural and class background, might see the photo and see the Project members as "good-time girls who aren't exactly bitter, yet" and who are demonstrating that politics can be fun. This interpretation might inspire them to get involved, which is how the University of Waterloo Chapter came into being. A group of students "read a *Toronto Star* article about us [in 2006] and they ... contacted the writer of the article to get our email address ... and said 'Hey, I want to be on board.'" However, age-group peers and high schools students from a different class or cultural background may see a relative homogeny in the dress and appearance patterns of the group and be less likely to see themselves as "fitting in," which could interrupt the potential for involvement. Men as well, may view this picture and assume they wouldn't belong in a group like this one since there were no men photographed at this event, possibly sending the message that this form of feminism doesn't apply to them.

Politicians might see this group as being willing to work with the system, since this "protest" was in fact a lobbying luncheon to which female MPPs were invited. In fact, while Miss G___ members and supporters paid $20 for their lunch, MPPs were not required to pay, making the luncheon a sort of "wine and dine" paid for by

PACKAGING A (NON)FEMINIST IMAGE ·

Miss G__ members themselves. The project's "fun and feminine" appearance may lead politicians to take them less seriously than they might take a group putting forth a more severe image, and the emphasis on the group's youth might make them seem like less of a political threat than an older, more established and better connected group. Of course, Miss G__ members do this on purpose as part of their "Trojan Containment" strategy, which has already been discussed. Because only female MPPs were invited to this event, male MPPs, including then-minister of education Gerard Kennedy, might have thought that equity in education for women is not a subject that affects them. To the everyday person reading the *Toronto Star* who might not have any connection to feminist politics, the photo shows attractive women having a great time on a beautiful day in the park. Although there are many feminist indicators in the picture, such as the "Miss Educated" sashes and the blue stockings, for many people who are not engaged with feminism, these could potentially be missed. The accompanying article clearly uses delegitimizing frames to position Miss G__ as a "new," "fun" brand of unthreatening, good-looking feminism. The public is very likely to see the group as "good-time girls" on a mission to get a women's studies course into schools. They may or may not support this initiative based on their "reading" of the event and the group's politics, and they are unlikely to give the sort of public reaction against feminism that is typical in the mainstream culture. The main issue is that, because the group is depicted as being somewhat superficial, any support it gains from this coverage is likely to be superficial as well.

Of course, these possibilities for interpretation by different groups are all only possibilities and cannot be taken for granted. They are meant to illustrate the many current possibilities for better practice when it comes to presenting a cultivated public image.

Branding Miss G___

"I MIGHT NOT BE A FEMINIST, BUT": STRATEGIC FEMININITY AND BACKLASH POLITICS

If you don't name something as feminist, it stands a much greater chance of being accepted.

— Keely Savoie, "Unnatural Selection: Questioning Science's Gender Bias"

The Miss G___ Project's strategic use of femininity may be a useful way of presenting its goals without suffering from a feminist backlash like the one of the 1980s. As the quote above says, "If you don't name something as feminist, it stands a much greater chance of being accepted" (Savoie 2006, 139). Since meaning is created as much through what people explicitly say they are and how they appear to be, looking unlike the stereotypical feminist may be as good for gaining public support as saying that you are not one. Ghabrial mentioned that "even women who don't feel connected to feminism, but who like looking at strong women ... have been, for the most part, very excited for us." The fact that Miss G___ is able to appear attractive and can be interpreted as "strong women" rather than "strong feminists" may increase their public palatability, if not their reputation for meaningful politics.

Over the course of my interviews, I noticed a shocking trend of treating the term "feminist" as "the F word." While the members of the Miss G___ Project all consider themselves to be feminists, and privately they do define Miss G___ as a feminist endeavour, they each mentioned how their own families and social networks depoliticize "women's studies" and refuse to use the feminist label to describe Miss G___'s work. This was sometimes used consciously by Miss G___ members as a political strategy, for example in "marketing" the project to different members of the provincial parliament or to financial contributors. It seemed that the Project knew some of their well-moneyed and well-connected supporters felt more comfortable giving their time and money to a group of "women who care about equity in education" than to "feminists," even though these are inextricably connected to the group. Perhaps because of the group members' own socio-economic status and the tendency for wealthy people to support traditional politics, their networking base has been built up by a good deal of politically conservative people who are not comfortable with what one past supporter termed "radical feminism" seeping into the Miss G__ Project. Project members discuss their strategic deployment of the term "feminism":

Shdorkoff: It depends on who we're marketing it to.
Rawal: Yeah.
Shdorkoff: If we're marketing it to ...
Rawal: ... (Conservative MPP) Elizabeth Witmer, for example, who doesn't call herself a feminist ...
Shdorkoff: ... we play it down. If it's (Liberal MPP and current minister of education) Kathleen Wynne, we play it up.
Mohan: Right.
Shdorkoff: And that's going to get even more interesting now as we approach people to get money, because that's going to be very important. Donors who aren't uncomfortable with [feminists], we're not going to [be explicit about calling ourselves feminists]. If we're going to get money, we're going to [have to] tone it down, I think.

The group believes that sometimes it is strategic not to wear their feminist identification on their sleeves. One member explains, "If [anyone] ever said outright, 'Are you a feminist?' we'd say 'Yes, absolutely.' But [if] it's mainstream media [we're talking to], we're not going to wear it on our sleeves at that point." They believe that sometimes the issue of whether or not this is a feminist endeavour isn't relevant to the Project's coverage. In these circumstances, if articulating a feminist standpoint is going to alienate potential supporters, it may not be worth doing. Some people may believe that this approach abandons feminist principles and acquiesces to an anti-feminist mainstream, but Project members believe it to be smart lobbying.

In some cases, this depoliticizing of women's studies, from feminist to concerned citizen, comes from a need for their family and

Branding Miss G__

friends to separate the Project's members from their own negative conception of feminists. This creates an interesting disruption to the metaphor that third wave feminists are the daughters and sons of second wave activists. The truth is that many third wave feminists grew up in conservative homes, with parents who were extremely uncomfortable with the feminist label.

> *Rawal*: My dad [says], "I think it's a great thing that you're dong, this Miss G__ Project," and [I say], "Yeah, isn't feminism wonderful?" and [he says], "It's not feminism," and [I say], "Dad, it's clearly a feminist organization," and [he says], "That's not feminist, but it's a good thing you're doing."
>
> *Mohan*: Yeah, my dad said the same thing, because I was showing my parents some underwear I bought for my sister that said "Feminist" on it and my dad looks at it and said, "That's not good." So we sort of sparked this conversation and my dad [says], "I think that the work you're doing, like getting women's studies in is great, but feminism ... that's not good. That's when women hate men."

Of course, the media's fascination with the physical appearances of feminists is nothing new. Whether women are using their appearance to seek out more positive attention for their cause (like the Miss G__ Project posing for the *Toronto Star*), or using their looks as an entry point to expose exploitation in the workplace (like Gloria Steinem writing about Playboy Bunnies), or simply smeared in the press because their physical appearances deviate from the social ideal (like Betty Friedan), the media is quick to detail feminist women's hairstyles — on their heads, in their armpits or on their legs — with at least as much intensity as they are feminist women's political campaigns. Just as attractive women are given more positive attention in the mainstream culture, so are attractive feminists given more and better attention in the mainstream press. The popular historical understanding of "feminist glamazons" Gloria Steinem and Naomi Wolf are substantially different and far more positive than the less popular and less conventionally attractive Andrea Dworkin, who was truly vilified in the press for her appearance — she was frequently photographed in unflattering overalls — and her radical feminist stance. Of course, the more positive reception to more attractive feminists is often accompanied by "pigeon holing," wherein "good looking" feminists are good looking first and feminist second.

The feminist artist collective, the Guerilla Girls, commented on the media's obsession with good-looking feminists in their 2001 poster created as a fake advertisement for the faux-film *The Birth of Feminism*. The film gave credit to the birth of the women's movement to the very attractive Gloria Steinem, Flo Kennedy and Bella Abzug, played by Pamela Anderson, Halle Barry and Catherine Zeta-Jones, all of whom appear in bikinis. The byline for the faux-film is "They make women's rights look good. Really good" (2001, n.p.).

This can be alienating for feminists who are more interested in being "serious" than "sexy." This may seem like a strange statement, since surely all feminists want to be taken seriously. However, it should be noted that one of the most popular criticisms levelled against third wave feminists is that they are inordinately concerned about looking good, and not concerned enough with politics. In 2005, Jennifer Wells wrote an introductory article for the Miss G__ Project in the *Toronto Star*. Wells only mentions the feminist politics of the group in terms of the comments on "an impossibly idiotic white tube top, made for an 8-year-old or so [with] silver glitter on the thing and various [consumerist] sayings covering its front," which has Miss G__ members worrying about "the countervailing influences for girls and young women moving through the school system," but she does mention that "[Shdorkoff is] wearing big silver hoop earrings and a silver belt and great shoes and you just know that 'fun' is something that [she] does well." This did not escape the notice of a supporter from the Ontario Secondary School Teachers' Federation who sarcastically commented to Shdorkoff later that "I love how they mentioned your shoes."

According to Newman and White (2006), a majority of Canadian men and women are unwilling to identify themselves as feminists and are unwilling to ally themselves with movements

Branding Miss G__

they identify as feminist. This trend is similar to that in the United States. A Feminist Majority Foundation national poll taken in 1995 revealed that while 41 percent of women considered themselves feminist (quite a high percent, actually), that number rose to 67 percent when "feminist" was explicitly defined to be "someone who supports political, economic and social equality for women" (6–7). Newman and White believe that this points to a problem not with the principles of feminism but rather with the label itself, and specifically, what the label has come to represent in the public imagination — namely, hairy, scary and angry women out to take away the rights from "decent folk." I discuss above how some family members of the steering committee choose not to associate the work of their daughters as "feminist" work, since their understanding of "feminism" is not at all positive. While some people can divorce their understanding of "feminism" from their understanding of "women's studies," this knee-jerk reaction sometimes extends itself to efforts to adopt a women's studies curriculum, with some critics complaining that "the politics of feminism is about castrating and taking rights away from men [and] the purpose of women's studies courses ... is to 'bash' [and exclude] men" (see Newman & White 2006, 7–8).

These negative connotations — which have infiltrated the Canadian public imagination — can be attributed to a large degree to the negative media coverage feminists have often received, especially in the U.S. The popular image of a feminist may be as demonizing as Pat Robertson's often-quoted lament that feminism is "a socialist, anti-family political movement that encourages women to leave their husbands, kill their children, practice witchcraft, destroy capitalism, and become lesbians" (qtd. in Jervis & Zeisler 2006, 106). Sadly, Robertson's misguided beliefs about feminism are still prevalent in the media, albeit they are usually much less explicitly stated. This related locally to what Project members described as their parents' views of feminism: "feminism, that's not good ... that's when women hate men." Some feminists, including Miss G__ members, see these negative opinions as an inevitable and unfortunate behemoth that can and should be avoided through strategic use and concealment of ties to the feminist label. In the short term, this may help individual feminist groups achieve some level of success. However, going along with a backlash-fuelled public understanding of feminists does no good to the movement in the long run. Carol Rivers (1996) believes that, despite the bad press feminism has gotten in the past, it is vital to the women's movement that feminists maintain a proud use of this term. "The word is important, because without it women have no history, the accomplishments of women can be presented as simply those of isolated individuals and the opposition to the progress downplayed ... those who forget their history are condemned to repeat it" (112–113).

Despite the fact that overdisplays and exaggerated pronouncements of feminist identity may cause some alienation in mainstream culture, I believe it is immensely problematic to drop the term "feminism" in order to increase palatability. This palatability leads to a depoliticization of the women's movement, which is troublesome for the Project, because apolitical lobbying is likely to lead to an apolitical "women in history" survey-type course that doesn't challenge gender inequality structurally. In fact, this kind of course would be merely an extension of the "sidebar" approaches to teaching women's issues that schools are already using. "Sidebar" refers to the small coloured boxes in a history book where the history of women, ethnic minorities, immigrants, and possibly queer or disabled people are relegated. Anyone who has recently taken a high-school-level history class is familiar with this approach to integrating "multiple voices" into the curriculum, while at the same time positioning them as "extra." An apolitical women's studies course would be merely a 76-minute "sidebar" to an otherwise business-as-usual school day. The Project's goal is for a transformational course that challenges privilege and leads students to think critically and to apply feminist theory to the structural inequalities that face them daily. Members expressed concern in our interviews that the course they have proposed would "[get] into the wrong hands," resulting in the kind of survey course I have discussed. However, despite the worry that the course may be developed and taught in a non-feminist way, they seemed uncritical about what their role in this depoliticization might be. They did not connect their willingness to "play [feminism] down" in their lobbying efforts with the possibility that feminism would be "played down" in the course itself.

Although group members acknowledged that even having a woman teaching the course would not ensure that it was being delivered in a feminist way, when I asked whether they envisioned the course to be feminist, they responded uncritically that "I think it's inherently a feminist [course]" and "I think even having the concept of a women's studies course is a feminist [one]." This contradiction jeopardizes the goals of the Project at the same time that it increases its potential for success. I believe that to depoliticize feminism in order to better market it is troublesome, and it should be avoided. Bonnie Dow (1996) argues, "It would be nice if the majority of women in this country felt comfortable saying 'Yes, I am a feminist'; but if the way to make that happen is to empty the term of all political implications so that all it really means is 'I like myself,' then feminism has not gained much" (213).

It may be true that a feminist project such as Miss G__ could get a better reception in the mainstream by appearing apolitical and therefore unthreatening. However, by compromising the appearance of feminism, we must ask if we are compromising feminism itself.

PACKAGING FEMINISM: TWO STUDIES

As much as we long for a society in which substance overrides style, in our media driven age, image and appearance are undeniably important ... even among self-identified feminists.

— Heather E. Bullock and Julian Fernald, "'Feminism Lite?'"

At least two studies have been undertaken to determine the effect of "packaging" on the political and social identity of feminists. The common reluctance to portray an overtly feminist image in the media stems partially from the findings of studies such as Leonie Huddy's 1998 investigation into women's political self-identification. Huddy asked female participants to read an article about the women's movement that carried a photo of a white female feminist. This photo was altered to represent different career orientations and levels of traditional femininity, but each news article had exactly the same text. Participants were spilt into four groups and asked to rate their identification with feminism before and after reading the same text with a randomly assigned photo. As a result of this research, Huddy reconceptualized political self-identity as an extension and reflection of social identity, concluding that political self-identification reflects both one's intellectual beliefs and a desire to be allied with the types of people who are thought to identify with that specific ideology. This conclusion is far from groundbreaking, especially in the realm of feminism, where self-defined membership in the movement has long suffered from "I'm not a feminist, but ..." syndrome, fed by many women's reluctance to consider themselves members of a group full of frightening feminist women. Oftentimes a reluctance to self-identify as a feminist will be accompanied by a belief in feminist ideologies and an appreciation of feminist social gains, proving that what people have problems with is the label or the identity of feminist rather than the movement itself.

Huddy (1998) surveyed black and white women in the U.S. and found white women were more likely to identify with women who appeared to have the same career orientation as they had rather than with their degree of femininity. The reverse was true for black women, for whom the degree of femininity was a better determinant. Surprisingly, Huddy found that well-educated white women were most likely to align themselves politically according to their personal feelings about what people associated with ideologically rather than according to their own intellectual agreement. Huddy believes that her research on feminist identity proves the importance of a "group protocol in conveying information about political groups and political identity" (7). This protocol should be consistent with or complementary to the kinds of supporters the group hopes to gain (9). She believes that when considering political identification, lay people assess themselves against the representations of group members who are already established, asking, "Are they my kind of people? Do I fit in?" (8).

The results of Huddy's (1998) study are similar to those of Heather Bullock and Julian Fernand (2003), who surveyed a group of mainly middle-class, mainly white and mainly heterosexual students from Lincoln, Nebraska, to investigate whether they would respond more favourably to a feminist message if the messenger appeared to share their personal class and sexual identity. They believed that female undergraduates responded more positively to instructors who presented themselves in a traditionally feminine way, wearing flattering clothing and makeup, with styled hair, even within the realm of women's studies. They termed this phenomenon "feminism lite," understanding it as "the idea that feminism is more palatable when the messenger's physical appearance does not directly challenge traditional standards of femininity" (291). Results of their study provided strong support for this concept (295).

Neither of these studies presents surprising conclusions. The strategy these findings imply is widely disseminated in activist handbooks for feminists and non-feminists alike (see, for example, Wilson 2001; Ryan 1992). When lobbying for the support of a specific portion of the population, it is strategically intelligent to appear as much as possible like members of that group. Take, for example, Canadian Green Party leader Elizabeth May's (2006) advice on activists staffing tables in malls: "Ideally, your volunteers ... are dressed conventionally ... Appealing to the average shopper you need to look like the average shopper. Your mall table is not a place to send your blue-haired, multi-tattooed and pierced volunteers" (89).

Of course, the findings of these studies don't point to absolute truths for how to effectively curry favour with one group. For example, educational administrators may prefer a professional and apparently apolitical approach, but this same approach could be ineffective and alienating to a radical teachers' group which may share my views that feminism should be explicitly feminist. This is precisely the problem feminist groups run into — alienating either mainstream or "fringe" supporters with their cultivated public image. When synthesizing strategically important information into a group's lobbying plan, it is important to maintain the group's integrity at all times. Compromises over appearance that dilute a group's vision or message are never effective for lobbying; even if more supporters are gained, their support is only superficial, based on the compromised information they were presented initially and not on the reality of the group's standpoint.

These two studies and May's (2006) advice affirm a basic fact of lobbying: that potential supporters and participants are more likely to want to join or support a group whose members remind them of themselves. Miss G__ members are aware of this, and acknowledge that they seem "very one way," meaning feminine, middle-class and "functionally white" (which will be discussed in depth in chapter 4.) This term refers to Miss G__ members' ethnicities being downplayed by reporters and photographers in the press. It seems to members that because they aren't "African Canadian" or "Asian enough" some people look right past their ethnicities and consider them to be white "for all intents and purposes." This happens on both sides of the political spectrum. Miss G__ members have noticed that in some of Toronto's feminist circles certain Project members' ethnicities are scoffed at. Mohan, who is perhaps the most visible minority in the Project, discussed an interview she had with some women from a popular feminist bookstore in Toronto. "They said, 'How do you negotiate being a woman of colour and the kind of white second wave feminism the Miss G__ Project is working with?' That really caught me off guard, the assumption that my energy wasn't shaping the work we were doing, and that these women we thought were so with it didn't understand what we were doing." Rawal explained further, "That really is more of a betrayal than the conservatives [who think we're radical lesbians] because they're not even trying to understand and we really believe in having meetings and discussions. We would love to sit down and have those discussions."

If Huddy, Bullock and Fernand, and May are right, and the

Branding Miss G___

public is more likely to support a group that is similar to themselves, it makes sense that a group's image should reflect as broad a segment of society as possible. The Miss G___ Project realizes the importance of visibly diversifying but are aware that in doing so could result in the tokenism they see as more befitting the second wave. They wish to appear more diverse "without lapsing into the 'Liberal ad' where you have your token black person, your token Asian, your token disabled person." Of course, their perception that this self-defined third wave endeavour needs to appear more diverse runs in contradiction with their previously articulated belief that within the third wave, and unlike the second, diversity is inherent. The reluctance to fall into a "Liberal ad" also contradicts their statement that one token lesbian on the steering committee — maybe two — would be okay. Understand that I'm not criticizing Miss G___ members' intention, only their short-sightedness on these issues. Part of the problem with the messiness of the third wave is the difficulty of making statements that are "true" in all circumstances. I believe that this media approach needs to become more self-critical, so that Project members can better analyze the messages they put out, instead of being surprised when they learn how these messages are being taken up in the public sphere.

CHANGING THE WORLD BY PLAYING THE GAME

I'm disturbed by the push for alliance with the corporate boardroom and not the union hall.
— Joanna Kadi, *Thinking Class*

The Miss G___ Project chooses to use its "lobbying" as a way to ap peal to the powerful and influential, and not to the weak and the vulnerable. The members create a public image that appeals to those in similar and better social and political positions than they hold but which may alienate those with more of a middle-class/lower-class social standing. This can be understood as "playing the game," and it certainly is a safe strategic choice. It is a choice to use a privileged class and educational background in order to connect on a personal and professional level with the politicians and professionals who may be of the most use to the group. This choice might be a result of the members feeling most comfortable approaching groups who share a similar cultural background. Of course, the Project is supported by several unions, including the Ontario Secondary School Teachers' Federation (OSSTF) and the Canadian Auto Workers (CAW), and is frequently asked to give presentations at union meetings and conferences. So, it is not as if Project members ignore these kinds of groups, but rather that some of the ways they choose to present their initiative is intended to attract a different support base.

This choice is "smart" because it allows Project members to make political connections now which can serve them in their future careers and endeavours; it may, however, require them to "play nicely" with the Ministry of Education. An example of the Project's desire to go with, rather than against the ministry, occurred in the fall of 2006. A meeting with the current minister of education, Kathleen Wynne, had been set up a number of times but kept falling through, leaving the group's members to worry that their concerns were being put on the back burner, despite their friendly and supportive relationship with Wynne. A suggestion was offered to the group that they stage a sit-in at Queen's Park, demanding to be seen by the minister, and invite media. This suggestion was vetoed, because of the members' concerns that the members of the ministry "get their backs up when they think we're going to make them 'look bad'" (personal communication with the Miss G__ Project, November 6, 2006). This reasoning can be termed a "dutiful daughter" approach, and one to which the Miss G__ Project attributes much of its success. However, it must be acknowledged that groups and individuals that have a vested personal, professional or political interest in staying on the ministry's "good side," or maintaining positive relationships with donors, is at a disadvantage when it comes to taking risks in lobbying (see, for example, Schroeder 2003, 34).

After the Read-In, the Miss G__ Project received an email from a one-time donor and supporter with a political background who had initially done a lot of work to help the Project network with MPPs.

Branding Miss G__

The supporter was unhappy about the event and the direction in which the Project was heading. Although a focus on combating homophobia had always been part of Miss G__'s explicit mandate, this donor-supporter believed that "the Miss G__ Project committee, which was a very vibrant group of young political activists with a very exciting project, has been taken over by radical feminists and a gay, lesbian, bisexual lobby group" (personal email to the Miss G__ Project, October 5, 2006). Miss G__ members were shocked to receive this email for several reasons. The first was that everyone involved thought that the Read-In was a very tame, relaxed event. While it was more "radical" than the previous "New Girls' Club Luncheon," it was still very much a "dutiful daughter" lobbying choice, with the minister of education herself reading India Arie lyrics to Miss G__ members. This really led the group to question whether they were gaining the kind of support they were hoping for, and whether they were being explicit and up front enough about their politics. This is clearly one of the major problems with taking a relatively apolitical approach to feminist lobbying — a dilution of a group's politics. After much deliberation, the group decided not to let this woman's criticisms affect its lobbying or influence the goals of the initiative itself. In response, the group addressed the blatant homophobia in the complaint: "We are saddened by the thought that our advocacy for education on, and an understanding of, the struggles and injustices suffered by those who identify as gay, lesbian, bisexual, transgendered, intersexed, or any other label, would cause you to withdraw your support" (personal email from the Miss G__ Project, October 6, 2006). They decided that the group was better off without the help of people whose politics didn't accord with the basic principles of educational equity.

The label "dutiful daughter" is used both in the context of the women's movement and the wider political sphere. Within the movement, many third wave feminists are accused of being "undutiful daughters" by older feminists, who believe that young feminists are "careerists ... who are not political enough — not sufficiently grateful to the past generation for fighting the battles that made today's lives possible" (Looser & Kaplan 1997, ix). This criticism, which has elsewhere been referred to as "blind obedience syndrome" (Elm 1997, 62), is complex. To be a dutiful daughter within the feminist movement is seen as radical in the realm of public politics, as it requires more radical forms of feminist activism, such as the sit-ins that might make the ministry "look bad." Many of the ways young feminists "act out" undutifully within the feminist movement are incredibly "dutiful" to the present political order, relying on "playing the game" to achieve political successes rather than demanding change where it is due.

Project members are right in believing that this dutiful daughter approach to working with the ministry has been successful in gaining government support, as the group did succeed in getting a positive meeting with Wynne in February of 2007. Soon after, Miss G__ was awarded a $70,000 grant to develop teaching resources; these funds were granted through the past minister of education's (Sandra Pupatello) "women in education" fund. However, the perceived importance of having a friendly relationship with the ministry places restrictions on the types of activism with which this group can engage. At the present, Miss G__ members are becoming frustrated that their "good relationship" hasn't yielded any serious consideration for a women's studies course. Although, at their February 2007 meeting, members were left believing that by fall of 2008 two new courses would be added to the curriculum: one on the environment and one on women's studies, which they had been suggesting for years. A panel of experts was put together over the summer of 2007 to discuss what this women's studies course would look like. The Miss G__ steering committee was asked to submit a list of people they thought would be best to help plan this course, which they did. Unfortunately, not one of these individuals, which included feminists from across Ontario with myriad connections to women's studies, myself included, was considered. Miss G__ members attempted repeatedly to get in touch with their designated contact person in the ministry over the summer, to little success.

In September of 2007, the environment course was announced

Branding Miss G___

by ministry officials, and Miss G___ members waited to hear about the women's studies course. Their calls to the ministry were not returned. Eventually they found out third hand from one member's family friend that the course was not being approved. Miss G___ members were very frustrated by the lack of transparency they saw in the ministry. Although the steering committee doesn't have any animosity for the ministry and still looks forward to a good working relationship with ministry officials, they are disappointed. As Ghabrial said, "We spent so much time cultivating a relationship with the ministry, which ended up being so one-sided. We put in so much effort and they didn't help at all." Unfortunately, by "playing nice" with the ministry, Miss G___ members may have made themselves easy to ignore.

A political approach where women can only be as political as is palatable for the government and the mainstream public can negatively influence the fruits of a group's labour. For Miss G___, this would mean the adoption of a women's studies course that looks nice but does not challenge the status quo. This possible depoliticized "dutiful daughter" version of a women's studies course is, I believe, worse than no women's studies course at all. The institution of a women's studies course without a distinctly feminist foundation is not a politically neutral possibility. As Lisa Jervis (2005b) points out, to elect non-feminist women into politics in order to increase the number of women in power is a trap. She argues,

> Having a woman in the White House won't necessarily do a damn thing for progressive feminism ... women who do nothing to enact feminist policies will be elected and backlash will flourish. I can hear the refrain now: "They've finally got a woman in the White House, so why are feminists still whining about equal pay?" (n.p., see also Bromley & Ahmad 2006, 66)

This is precisely the problem with creating a non-feminist women's studies course, because it could encourage the refrain, "They've finally got a women's studies course in the curriculum, why are all those feminist teachers still whining about challenging the status quo?" Rebick and Roach (1996) discuss the process of governments institutionalizing feminist goals:

> The problem has been, as soon as you get to the point where the government starts to recognize that they have to deal with the issue, a process of co-option begins. The result is ... the professionalization of our issues, dressing them up in language and demands that government bureaucrats, politicians and the media can accept ... Our demands change from affirmative action to employment equity, and our tactics change from using the streets to relying on committee rooms. (96)

I know that members of the Miss G__ Project would be disturbed and disappointed if a course they lobbied so passionately for disrupted rather than created the potential for real feminist change, and yet I worry that some aspects of their lobbying may contribute to this potentiality.

The problem with an image-related media strategy such as the one used by Miss G__ is that while emphasizing femininity and flirtatiousness in the press might be successful at gaining the attention of mainstream media outlets such as the *Toronto Star*, the message that's actually getting across might contradict the goals the group has established. In the next chapter, I discuss Miss G__'s media coverage in detail, according to how the articles and photos were organized and staged, whether framing devices were used to delegitimize the group and to what effect. I also give suggestions for a media practice that may ensure a greater consistency between what is intended and what is being communicated.

Miss G__ members (foreground from left: Kathryn Mitrow, Lara Shdorkoff, Dilani Mohan, Sheetal Rawal, Sarah Ghabrial, Michelle Miller) pose with croquet mallets for the *Toronto Star* at the "New Girls' Club Luncheon."

Sheetal Rawal, Jenna Owsianik, Joy Cowell and Sarah Ghabrial pose in their "Miss Education" sashes at Queen's Park during the "New Girls' Club Luncheon."

— HOLLY KENT

Miss G__ supporters spread out on the lawn at Queen's Park for the June 6 Read-In.

— MICHELLE MILLER

Jill Barber playing at the June 6 Read-In.

— MICHELLE MILLER

Sarah Ghabrial, Lara Shdorkoff, Laurel Mitchell, Rhea Mitchell, Sandy Kulchar, Danielle Longfield, Dilani Mohan, Holly Kent and Sheetal Rawal curled up with the Miss G__ logo at the June 6 Read-In.

Jenna Owsianik, Sarah Ghabrial, Lara Shdorkoff, Sheetal Rawal and Dilani Mohan admiring the patriarchs at the University of Toronto's Hart House during the *Shameless* magazine shoot.

Sheetal Rawal, Lara Shdorkoff, Dilani Mohan, Sarah Ghabrial and Jenna Owsianik doing some light reading at Hart House.

— Amanda Rataj

Dilani Mohan, Lara Shdorkoff, Jenna Owsianik, Sarah Ghabrial and Sheetal Rawal making a mess at Hart House.

Dilani Mohan, Lara Shdorkoff, Jenna Owsianik, Sarah Ghabrial and Sheetal Rawal at Hart House.

— Shae Gowland

A Miss G__ supporter holds a powerful message at Queen's Park on February 14, 2008.

Chapter 4
TRACKING MEDIA REPRESENTATIONS

GAINING MEDIA ATTENTION HAS LONG BEEN AN IMPORTANT ASPECT of the Miss G__ Project's lobbying approach. As a new lobbying initiative, members believe it to be extremely important that the Project gain a public and political profile, attract more donors, gain more support and put more pressure on political figures to institute the women's and gender studies course for which they are lobbying. In fact, they consider the amount of media coverage they've attracted to be one of the Project's main successes. Mohan explains, "I think the fact that we were able to get the media that we've gotten [is a huge success]. Activist groups and feminist groups especially don't get much coverage and aren't generally represented very well, and so for us even to have gotten as much as we have is something amazing." Miss G__ members have been accused of being both "media savvy" and "media darlings." Shdorkoff did her Bachelor of Arts in Media Information Technology at UWO, and other group members have experience with and connections to media outlets, reporters and editors.

In many instances, Miss G__ members contacted the newspapers and CBC Radio, requesting interviews and profile pieces. Particularly at first, members used their connections to get media attention, and even went so far as to ask the *Toronto Star* to take their picture, because they knew it would attract readers to the article about them. Initially, Sarah Ghabrial did most of the media work, although from 2006, much of the responsibility of contacting the media has been shared with Laurel Mitchell. Part of the members' savvy is their willingness to go out on a limb, contacting papers and requesting attention, and then gearing their interviews and lobbying events to attract the support of the paper or reporter in question. When it comes to the feminist media, this approach hasn't been necessary. Most of the positive profiles of the group have come from the feminist or leftist media and have been "published in more diverse popular press outlets" (Ashley & Olson 1998, 274) that include *Shameless, Herizons* and, most recently, *McClung's*, a feminist magazine based out of Ryerson University, and the progressive education journal *Our Schools / Our Selves*.

COMING OUT: THE TORONTO STAR

> *Feminism is not dead — it goes to university and wears buttons like "My short skirt and everything under it is Mine!"*
> — Louise Brown, "Young Feminists on a Mission"

A *Toronto Star* article on July 23, 2005, served as Miss G__'s formal "coming out." Written by Jennifer Wells, this story introduced the group to the mainstream public; they were hoping to broaden their political profile and recruit some supporters and donors. When the Project first came together in 2005, Sarah Ghabrial was doing most of the media work, calling papers and the CBC and asking for coverage, but in this case it was a member's personal connection to an editor at the *Star* that facilitated the interview. This is one of the great benefits of a group with strong social capital networks. Miss G__ members seem to be "connected" to the "right" people to get their message out. The article, which was published in the *Star*'s "Life" section, was conversational in tone and felt like a profile in a women's magazine. While this approach was fun to read, it created the impression that the story wasn't "hard news." This kind of conversational tone is popularly used in women's interest articles, so while the article would likely attract a high female readership, it reduced the possibility of attracting a male readership. When introducing the Project's namesake, Wells wrote, "You're bound to ask who the heck is Miss G. [*sic*]? It's been way too hot this week to grapple with puzzles and changes are darned slim that Miss G. [*sic*] will ring any bells." She went on to describe Dr. Clarke's *Sex in Education* as "a hot, hot seller," in a very quick and very cutsie retelling of Miss G__'s story.

Not unsurprisingly, considering Bronstein's (2005) research that the mainstream media portrays third wave feminists as "look[ing] great and transform[ing] the fiery ideological character of the second wave into a friendly and approachable, but less substantive brand of feminism," this article opened with a comment about the steering committee's dress and sense of fun: "Four young women blow into the newsroom borne by way more levity than the place is used to. Each wears a T-shirt, each T a different colour and emblazoned with the modernized likeness of Miss G. [*sic*], replete with upswung hair and funky glasses" (Wells 2005). The article's appraisal of the Miss G__ Project was positive and appeared to celebrate the young women she referred to as "the fantastic four," whose dynamic personalities and "can do" spirit were admirable qualities that, she wrote, were missing both in feminism and in the younger generation. The four members of the steering committee were presented as "enthusiastic thinkers on a mission."

Near the end of the article, after outlining the Project's goals, Wells (2005) emphasized that one of the goals was to lobby in a way that is fun, such as having read-ins and doing culture jamming. She illustrated this drive for fun by quoting one of the members and describing her personality: "Says Shkordoff 'We want this to be visible and we want this to be fun.' She's wearing big silver hoop earrings and a silver belt and great shoes and you just know that 'fun' is something that Shkordoff does well." Wells did not mention that the group considers itself to be a feminist organization nor did she ask questions about the group's political standpoint and philosophy.

Branding Miss G___

— Keith Beaty, courtesy of the Toronto Star

The article was accompanied by a large photo of the four women in "cute and coy" poses, wearing their Miss G___ T-shirts. Some of the women were posed with their fingers in their mouths, looking up in a mock-bimbo "thinking pose." Others stood pigeon toed, with their hands on their hips, smiling sweetly into the camera. The group requested that their picture be published along with the article, and they chose the photo's tone, although the photographer posed them in these specific "girlie" images, which was in accordance with how Wells depicted them. The image in this article is the one they used in the press for the following year, and it illustrates precisely the public image the group cultivated in the beginning, with the emphasized femininity and flirty poses. It definitely reflected the overall tone of the story, and while it certainly attracted attention, it most likely disrupted the possibility of "hard news" readers giving it a second glance. Mohan explains why the group set this kind of mood for the photograph: "We had our little cheeky picture where we were sort of [performing] the ... idea [that] 'we [can be] little girls if that's how you want to treat us or [if] that's how you want to see us, but you know, we're actually doing something, so pay attention to this.'"

In the article, Wells appeared to support the Project and she presented the steering committee as a powerful force of fun and enthusiasm, if nothing else. However, despite her positive take on the Project, very little in the way she wrote presented them as legitimate political lobbyists. Whether purposefully or not, she used the standard media frames of personalization and feminism lite, both in tone and detail, in order to delegitimize the group. While the article appeared prominently in the paper and included a large photo, increasing the potential for readership, Wells did not present the group as a threat to the status quo. In fact, she wrote, "Not surprisingly, the Miss G. [sic] collective is not much interested in awaiting any formal curriculum review" (Wells 2005). While this may be intended to express the group's urgency to get a women's studies course into the curriculum quickly, the end result was that the Project was made to appear unaware of and unwilling to work with the processes necessary to achieve lobbying success. This depiction of the group's political short-sightedness, along with the frequent mentions of their enthusiasm and the photo, emphasized their youthfulness in a way that damaged their need to be taken seriously.

INTERVIEWING WITH THE ENEMY: *THE GAZETTE*

I call him lollipop, lollipop, oh, lolli lolli lolli.
— The Chordettes, *Lollipop*

The Miss G__ Project has been covered several times in UWO's campus newspaper *The Gazette*. It should be acknowledged that *The*

Branding Miss G__

Gazette has faced ongoing charges that its sexist and homophobic content is offensive to students, and annual campaigns to make the student levy that funds it optional rather than mandatory are ongoing and championed by supporters of Miss G__. One member of the Project had been engaged in an ongoing "media watch" and had written articles for other campus publications on the problematic material published in *The Gazette*. While coverage in campus news sources is important to any group's attempts to gather support within the school, the Miss G__ Project approaches coverage in this paper as a necessary evil, aware that a great deal of the paper's content is offensive and not remotely "news."

The first time the Project was covered in *The Gazette*, on September 22, 2005, the article was written in a surprisingly professional tone by the only male to yet report on the Project, Mitch Tucker. The article outlined the goals and background of the Project, carrying quotations from steering committee members and Dr. Rebecca Coulter, a professor in the Faculty of Education whom Miss G__ members have labelled "the Grand Matriarch of the Project." The article avoided using negative framing techniques and the group appeared to be professional, organized and confidently optimistic about their chances of success. It was published on the front page of the paper and carried a colour photo. Ultimately, the article was the ideal coverage for a new feminist project like Miss G__, although it did not explicitly cast the Project as feminist.

While the article was textually positive, the accompanying photo was problematic. It featured all four members of the steering committee behind a sign bearing the Miss G__ logo. The members appeared in their Miss G__ T shirts and whatever pants and shoes they had been wearing the day that the photo was taken. While their clothes were certainly nice, and members looked well-dressed and groomed, their body language did not read as "sexing it up" for the cause. The only really "cute" aspect of the photo was that Rawal had her hair up in two ponytails, but this was incidental. "I was between haircuts at the time," she explained in a 2006 interview. Their body language and casual dress clearly positioned them as everyday students on a regular school day. However, they were each posed with a lollipop either in their hands or in their mouths. These "lolli-props" were not referred to anywhere in the story; it appears they were used as a way to hint at the heterosexuality and desirability of the group's members — women sucking lollipops stands in for fellatio in popular sexual culture. It was the group's idea to use lollipops in this photo. They had used lollipops before, sending them out with their MPP information packages as a fun treat for those who took the time to read them. Given how much information MPPs receive everyday, placing a fun surprise in an information package is a common way for activist groups to make sure that their packages stand out and that their information gets seen. Miss G__ sent the Ministry of Education information about the group, frequently asked questions about women's and gender studies and curriculum suggestions for a women's studies course on pink paper, "and then we included a little lollipop in there ... which was cute."

The group's intention for *The Gazette* photo was to appear fun and cute while maintaining the image they had presented to the ministry, not to mention attracting potential readership by "sexing it up." However, posing with these lollipops not only sexualized Miss G__ members it also infantilized them, making them appear child-like and thus unthreatening. This objectification, sexualization and infantalization did not go unnoticed in UWO's community. One of Shdorkoff's classmates made a comment to her that the photo made it look as though they were coming off as being flirts and not as strong positive women. There is a saying that "a picture's worth a thousand words." In this case, the overt sexualization delegitimized the group, despite the positive textual coverage.

As I mentioned, posing with the lollipops was the group's idea, as it was in keeping with the fun and flirty image they were trying to put forward. Looking back, group members see this as an example of how uncritical they were of the ways they were portraying themselves and allowing themselves to be portrayed; they see it as an example of how they were "get[ting] carried away all the time." In my opinion, this is an example where using a coy and sexualized image delegitimized the group; the coverage would have been more positive had they not sexualized themselves through the use of coded props. It could be argued that this photo effectively expressed, as they put it, their "not exactly bitter, yet" image, which emphasized that Miss G__ members were fun and fun-loving, rather than strident and angry. This image may have gained them more support within the university itself; however, as Rawal pointed out, in retrospect, the members agreed they could never use this pose again, and, thankfully, it no longer reflects the group's ideal image.

THE *LONDON FREE PRESS* AND THE LOCAL EXCHANGE OF WOMEN

> *When PETA hoists a billboard or slaps up a glossy poster featuring a woman, you can bet she's unclothed or close to it ... a campaign promoting vegetarianism features the likes of Elizabeth "Showgirls" Berkley and Pamela Anderson dressed in lettuce-leaf bikinis and other scanty coverings made of salad fixings; the male rapper Common, however, appears with his shirt firmly on, holding a veggie burger.*
> — Rebecca Onion,
> "Tree so Horny: Can Sex Sell Environmentalism?"

On November 24, 2005, the Project was featured in the "City" section of the *London Free Press*. The article carried a very differently posed photo of the steering committee than what had been published in the *Toronto Star* and *Gazette*. In the *Free Press* photo, they appeared stoic and serious rather than fun, flirty and coy. It was clear that the photographer had never seen the Project's *Toronto Star* article, and it was also clear that he didn't understand the kind of article that his photo would accompany. The article itself was written by Kate Dubinsky, the paper's education reporter. It described steering committee members as being "incredulous" that their work might be successful, as "finishing each other's sentences" and speaking "with infectious conviction." The story was presented in a tone that approached "real news" but used subtle phrasing to distance the coverage from that of a serious news story. For example, when referring to the cross-party support the Project had gained from political figures, Dubinsky reported they had held meetings with "politicians of all stripes." The coverage relied on the personalization of the group, opening with a description of their personalities: "The four young women are full of enthusiasm and laughter." The story mentioned the group's strategic deployment of the term "feminist" due to stigmas associated with the "f-word," and while it hinted that group members considered themselves to be engaged in feminist work, it didn't explicitly cast them as being feminists.

This coverage was relatively straightforward. The group appeared likable and enthusiastic, a recurrent theme in news stories about the Project. Perhaps because Dubinsky had some knowledge of issues relating to education, the group also appeared well organized and knowledgeable. Dubinsky reported on both the group's expectations for the women's studies course and the local high school workshops they facilitated. Coverage like this could have been an excellent way to get the word out to teachers and principals in the London area about the workshops. The use of personalization in the article might have been a benefit rather than a detriment to the group since the coverage could have increased the potential of local area schools contacting the group based on their personalities, youth and vitality.

However, once again the photo accompanying the piece played a critical role. It was drastically different from the kind they had posed for earlier. The four young women were lined up diagonally close together, so that the photographer could capture their four faces, rather than their full torsos, even though the steering committee members wore their signature T-shirts. They were instructed not to look happy, cute or coy, but rather to just look the camera "in the eye." The group members were stricken by what they considered to be the strangeness of the photographer's requests:

Rawal: That *London Free Press* article was bizarre, the one that look[ed] like I've been beaten up, and Lara [was] in the front and then us and then Dilani [was] in the back.

Ghabrial: We all had our Miss G__ T-shirts on and we were

Branding Miss G

going to take a picture of the four of us, like the very girl group positions [we were doing at the time], and then he decided that he'd rather have the close up of our four faces. At first Dilani was in the front, and it was Dilani and then Sheetal and me and Lara, and then he move[d] Lara to the front and Dilani to the back. He said that Dilani's hair was getting in the way, and so he moved Lara to the front and Sheetal more to the back.

Rawal: He didn't have an excuse for that one; my face was getting in the way.

Ghabrial: So, just the four of us in a line, but adjusted so that Lara was in the front, so then our logo wasn't in the photo at all, it was just our faces and Sheetal just looked in the shadows, she looked beat up and sad and destitute. It was funny and not funny at the same time.

It seemed to group members that Shdorkoff was given "centre stage" because of her attractiveness, marketability and "whiteness." The group understands moves like this to be "part of the game" when it comes to using the media to promote them. They refer to this marketing as "subversion containment," meaning that they use their own attractiveness as a lure and then spread information about the Project while they have the attention their looks gain them.

Ghabrial: We've actually said that; let's exploit the capitalist technique, taking it down from the inside. It's what we stand against, especially images of women in the media; we look at misrepresentations of women. Lara and I have talked about how problematic women's images [can be] in the media and how should the Project work with that, how to subvert it.

Rawal: Use it [the fascination with good-looking women] and then lose it.

Ghabrial: Like using our marketability to get women's studies into the curriculum so that the next generation of young people who are going to be exposed to the media can read the media more critically.

Miller: Do you think that selling the project as a girl group is problematic?

Ghabrial: Well that's the thing, we know that when capitalism and patriarchy work together, women's bodies are used to sell products.

Miller: Even feminist products?

Ghabrial: Yeah, that's the thing, we see how that works and the process is to take a product and use women's bodies to sell it, that's the formula and our problems with that are manifold. But how can we use that to create a more aware generation of people?

I find this reasoning and this willingness to offer oneself as a feminist to a capitalist patriarchal society to be faulty. It cannot be possible that, in order to make gains for a movement that aims to end the oppression of women, feminists have to offer themselves and their bodies for sale on the capitalist patriarchal market. I believe this faulty reasoning is indicative of what Kathleen Hanna (2003) refers to as "all the crazy twists and turns that activism can take when it's trying to function within a mixed-up, patriarchal, capitalist framework" (136). When the capitalist framework tells you that looking good will gain you the kind of attention that may help to achieve feminist goals, it seems like a good idea to acquiesce with that for the greater good.

Of course, the Miss G__ Project is not the only activist initiative falling prey to these "crazy twists and turns" in our current social climate. The most obvious example of using female bodies to sell an activist agenda is likely the ongoing PETA campaign for "I'd rather go naked than wear fur," which features naked or nearly naked women with strategically placed vegetables and leaves covering their genitals. While Ghabrial notes that she neither agrees with or likes that campaign, I believe the philosophies between that and some of the marketing of Miss G__ in the mainstream media are similar, partially in intent, as the group does wish to be thought of as young and pretty media darlings, but mainly in the way the group is processed and interpreted in some mainstream media sources.

Branding Miss G___

THE BUSINESS OF WHITEWASHING: LONDON CITY LIFE

That London City Life *[picture] was so weird. It didn't look like us at all.*
— Sheetal Rawal

I have discussed above the ways that race played into the group's coverage in the *London Free Press*. It is interesting that the other media outlet where race and ethnicity play a major role in the Project's coverage was the only other coverage out of the City of London. The business magazine *London City Life* made the members of Miss G___ the "cover girls" of its February/March 2006 issue, accompanied by an article very strangely called "Nuthin' but a G Thang," possibly in a misguided attempt to play up the youth and "hipness" of the Project. In the cover photo, which carried a light bubblegum pink background uncommon to the usually straight-laced magazine, the four young women wore brightly coloured Miss G___ T-shirts and appeared distinctly "whitewashed." Ghabrial, who is Egyptian born, appeared as having pale porcelain white skin, while the rest of the group's members appeared "white" with a slight tan. There is no question that in editing each of the photos for this piece the group members were deliberately and specifically given whiter skin. Although the article itself only filled three and a half of the magazine's pages, it featured nine full-colour photographs — in addition to the cover — of the four Miss G___ members smiling broadly in their Miss G___ T-shirts. The backgrounds were bright, feminine colours that complemented the shades of the T-shirts, and each of the four women looked white, sweet and cute. This "photoshopped whiteness" was clearly an attempt by the magazine to promote a more palatable young feminist group to its readership. To achieve this would mean removing the negative connotations often associated with black and Middle-Eastern "others," through the process, often used in advertising, of "making white" where it is not.

Despite the fact that the bubblegum pink found on the cover was used throughout the article — along with other stereotypically feminine colours such as purple and light teal that invoked a mental image of a child's bedroom — the textual coverage by Cyndi Mills was positive. In her article, she discussed the goals, past work and achievements of the group in a professional, though conversational tone. The magazine is intended mainly for local business people and because they might have had the ability to donate money to the Project's cause, the article mentioned that the group accepted and required private funding (which could certainly have alleviated some of the group's financial stress). In this case, we need to understand media coverage in terms of "text and context" (Gabriel 1998, 20). Here, the text included illustrations that were digitally manipulated to enhance the whiteness of the article's subjects. Yet the context refers to the political and social climate in which the article was being published. More specifically, the context refers to the conservative social climate of London, Ontario, the socio-economic standpoint of the magazine's readers and the broader culture of prejudice and intolerance regarding "not-suitably white" citizens. If the magazine's editors believed that the group would receive funding from private commercial sources if they appeared as white, attractive young women, then this funding becomes problematic from a feminist standpoint that recognizes the intersections of race and sexism, and the importance of combating these oppressions.

When this article came out, Miss G__ members were surprised. "It didn't even look like us," Rawal reported. But as most members had never heard of the magazine at the time they were approached to be interviewed, they decided not to "make a big deal" out of it, despite their being disappointed and disgusted. "I think we were really getting an education [about how things are made to look in the media] in the beginning [of our lobbying]," Shdorkoff explained.

(NOT) ONLY FOR THE GIRLS: THE TORONTO STAR

Come closer. See how feminism can touch and change your life and all our lives. Come closer and know firsthand what feminist

*Branding Miss G_*

movement is all about. Come closer and you will see: feminism is for everybody.
— bell hooks, *Feminism Is for Everybody*

In 2006, the group began doing public lobbying actions, and their media coverage began to move away from profile pieces into reports on events. On March 30, 2006, the *Toronto Star* reported on the Project's "New Girls' Club Luncheon" at Queen's Park. The article was published in the "News" section of the paper and was written by Louise Brown. Despite its placement as a news story, the Project was again covered in a conversational tone, and once again the opening of the article referred to the appearance of the group members, along with the dreaded mention of the supposed death of feminism:

> Feminism is not dead — it goes to university and wears buttons like "My short skirt and everything under it is Mine!"
> The bold young faces — and bodies, for that matter — of the women's rights movement marched into Queen's Park yesterday with plenty of short skirts, long hair and cocky flair, to push politicians to make women's studies part of the high school curriculum. (A18)

Even with the use of delegitimizing personalization and feminism-lite frames, the article provided a fairly effective representation of the group's politics because it contained two mentions of political figures, specifically then minister of education Gerard Kennedy and the female MPPs from all three parties who lent their support to the cause. This gave some credence to the fact that lobbying for education reform is a political action, whether it is done by young women or — as it is more frequently done — by parents' groups. However, it is interesting to note that Brown treated the Project as a specifically female endeavour, reporting only that *female* MPPs and the minister of education support the Project, which concurrently makes the statement that a women's studies course in high school curriculum only affects women. This is something that the Project has stressed is untrue and is based on patriarchal misrepresentations of the movement:

As part of the backlash against anything that empowers women (like with saaaay, feminism), Women's & Gender Studies has sometimes been dismissed as a male-bashing fest. Women's & Gender Studies is not out to start Gender Wars: Venus vs. Mars ... though that would probably make a great Fox TV special. It's more interested in looking at a variety of topics while paying attention to gender, race, sexual orientation, and class. Many men take AND ENJOY (gasp!) Women's & Gender Studies courses, and find them eye-opening. (The Miss G__ Project 2007c, n.p.)

The article was accompanied by a large, full-colour photo of group members playing croquet on the lawns of Queen's Park, with some members wearing "Miss Educated" sashes and three members of the steering committee in blue stockings, with all four wearing vintage dresses. Everyone was smiling genuinely, having a great time on a very bright and mild March day. The group's fun-loving image in this photo was pre-planned to a large extent. Ghabrial had sent out a press release in advance and members knew that a *Toronto Star* reporter would be present. According to Shdorkoff, "For the luncheon, we knew that the *Toronto Star* was going to be there, and we knew that they knew us from before as the four flirty girls and we wanted to give them something similar to that." This photo brought a great deal of attention to the article, and for days later many members were inundated with emails and phone messages from people who had seen them in the paper. This is a good example of Miss G__ creating a newsworthy event to gain mainstream media coverage. However, as will be discussed later on in this chapter, most of the feedback from this event didn't do much to win the Project additional support.

ON BEING MISREAD: *THE TORONTO STAR*

How shall we ever make the world intelligent of our movement? I do not think that the answer lies in trying to render feminism easy, popular, and instantly gratifying. To conjure with the passive culture and adapt to its rules is to degrade and deny the fullness of our meaning and intention.
    — Adrienne Rich, *On Lies, Secrets and Silences*

Branding Miss G___

On June 7, 2006, the *Toronto Star* ran a mention of Miss G__'s June 6 Read-In at Queen's Park. Despite the fact that this lobbying event was attended by more supporters than the previous luncheon event, including then minister of education Sandra Pupatello and MPPs Kathleen Wynne (Ontario's current minister of education) and Deb Matthews, this event received far less coverage in the *Star* than was anticipated. Buried in the "R" section, the article carried a small photo showing the back of a group member wearing a T-shirt printed with "This Is What a Feminist Looks Like." This photo represented the first time a picture of the group wasn't staged, and the first time a photo was published without the steering committee being featured prominently. Members of the steering committee did not see this as a problem. In fact, by 2006, the Project was fairly established in the political sphere and the steering committee was beginning to change its image. As Shdorkoff explained at the time, "Our image [of four good-time gals] is a good marketing technique, we're a good face for it, but I don't want people to get the idea that we're the only ones working on the project, because we're not." While the steering committee wanted to have a consistent image in the beginning, they were starting to feel comfortable with non-steering committee members being photographed at events as well.

The *Toronto Star*'s Read-In article carried no byline and simply stated that the Read-In took place. The day-long event was covered in the following mention:

> Young women from across Ontario held a "read-in" on the front lawn of Queen's Park this week to boost their bid for a women's studies credit in high school.
>
> The Miss G__ Project organized the Tuesday event, which also included musical performances and poetry and book readings. It attracted some high-profile guests, including provincial Education Minister Sandra Pupatello.
>
> The Miss G__ Project is a group of mainly female students lobbying to have women's studies recognized as an optional Grade 11 or 12 course under the new provincial four-year curriculum.
>
> The name is a nod to the first American woman to attend university, known only as Miss G__, whose early death in 1873 was

blamed by doctors on the overuse of her brain.

Such a course could cover women's contributions to politics, history, the media, sports and arts, as well as feminism and violence against women. ("Read-In Boosts Bid for Women's Studies Credit" 2006, R09)

This coverage was surprising to the group. The Read-In was considered a success, illustrating the mood and politics of the group by combining a celebration of Canadian women's voices with an information and a lobbying session. Ghabrial explained, "[With the Read-In] we wanted to demonstrate literally what we think is missing from the current curriculum — feminist and queer-positive literature, and women's histories" (qtd. in Mitchell 2006, 22). It also provided an opportunity for chapter members from across the province to come together for the cause, which provided an excellent opportunity for networking and brainstorming.

While there could be numerous explanations for the lack of coverage of this event, it has been suggested by some members of the group that the event was more "radical" than their previous lobbying events, which might have made for less attractive pictures. Interestingly, despite the short length and poor placement of the article, it represented a shift for the better in the way the group had been featured up until then: in this article, the *Toronto Star* used a newsworthy tone to detail an action taken by the Project.

THE HIPSTER NEWS: *NOW* MAGAZINE

There are mothers with babies in T-shirts that read "Future feminist" and the occasional supportive boyfriend type. A gaggle of organizers clad in "This is what a feminist looks like" shirts get the sound system going ... the park starts to rock in an encouraging inoffensive women's studies kind of way.
— Zoe Whittall, "They Call Me Miss G"

With the Read-In, the Miss G__ Project began to attract more attention from a variety of newspapers and magazines, including Toronto's entertainment weekly, *NOW* magazine. "They Call Me Miss G" was written by Zoe Whittall, a well-known Toronto poet, novelist and journalist, and made it into the "News" section and carried a photo of group members Sheetal Rawal, Sarah Ghabrial, Laurel Mitchell and myself dancing on the lawn at Queen's Park. It was written in a conversational and somewhat sardonic tone, allowing Whittall to subtly distance herself from feminism while emphasizing the success of the event. In some places the coverage explicitly derided feminism, saying "the earnestness quotient [was] high." She referred to women's studies as "inoffensive," and opened the article with an all-too familiar mention of supporters' appearances, and went on to stress that the event experienced some technical difficulties: "I see a cluster of 50 or so well-dressed academics sitting in a haphazard semi-circle around a folksinger who's making do without a microphone while a nearby city worker trims the hedges loudly." Whittall's decision to refer only generally to the unnamed folksinger — in actuality the well-known and critically acclaimed songwriter Jill Barber, whose support and presence at the event was a huge honour for Miss G__ members — while very specifically outlining the group's organizational problems illustrates a framing technique often used to delegitimize grassroots groups as ineffectual and low budget. Whittall failed to mention that before long, the microphone was made to work and the hedge trimming was drowned out by the group.

Although this was the first article to mention that the group was supported by men as well as women, Whittall referred to the men present that day as "supportive boyfriend types," indicating that men who might support a women's studies initiative would do so not out of a personal interest in women's studies or educational equity but rather because their girlfriends wanted them to. While not quoting any of the men in the crowd, Whittall does quote then minister of education Sandra Pupatello, who referred to Miss G__ as "a group of energetic young women with high levels of self-esteem"; poet and participant A. Rawlings, who believed that her life would have been different with women's studies in high school, and said, "I was fortunate to have a librarian who brought me a Larissa Lai book in my final year, and it totally changed my idea of how I could write"; and feminist educator Shannon Mills, who said, "I designed my own women's studies course, but it would have been a lot easier if there had been a curriculum there." Their comments echo the article's overall positive take on the group, the accomplishments it has seen and its goals; however, when the group's actions became "too feminist," Whittall became uncomfortable, ending her coverage by saying, "As the crowd grows, a young woman with the word 'brazen' painted on her arm urges participants to knit or make crafts in the crafting area or come to the mic to read. I leave before agonizing memories of early-90s open-mic nights overcome me" (n.p.).

This subtle distancing may be expected when women reporters are ghettoized to report on feminist initiatives, if the reporters don't identify or wish not to be identified as such. In a patriarchy, women are rewarded for making anti-feminist statements and allying themselves against movements for women's rights, and some women, especially those in typically male professions such as journalism and politics, often deride feminists in order to obtain some of the second-hand power that comes from male approval.

AN EDITOR OF OUR OWN:
THE HURON GRAPEVINE

Freedom of the press belongs to the man who owns one.
—Judy Rebick, *Ten Thousand Roses*

The Gazette is not the only campus news source at the University of Western Ontario. *The Huron Grapevine*, coming out of Huron University College, a UWO affiliate, represents a more left-leaning approach to Western's news. Priding itself on covering political stories, carrying informed and subversive editorials and edgy creative writing and photography, the magazine quality of *The Grapevine* makes it a popular choice for those students who are opposed to *The Gazette*. Laurel Mitchell, one of *The Grapevine*'s co-editors and member of The Miss G__ Project, covered the Read-In extensively in the Summer 2006 issue. The front cover featured a picture

Branding Miss G_

of Rawal under the headline "The Next Generation of Feminists." Inside, ten full pages were devoted to the event, accompanied by full-colour photos of the day's participants. Carrying quotations from Judy Rebick, Sandra Pupatello, various supporters as well as the steering committee, Mitchell's coverage was relevant and positive. This was to be expected, given that Mitchell was engaged with the Project and helped to organize the event. I think that this situation points to an important reality in feminist lobbying: when feminist and politically supportive journalists cover events, they are more willing to take time and care in giving the initiative balanced coverage. They also make a point of adding important and relevant information. For example, Mitchell's article carried a sidebar of frequently asked questions about the Project. One of the questions was, "Is women's studies 'for girls' only?" to which Mitchell responded, "Women's studies is for women, men and everyone in between" (Mitchell 2006, 29), which is interesting when compared with other coverage that positioned women's studies as a specifically female concern.

This was clearly the most positive and effective media coverage the Project had seen at the time. Far from acquiescing with the patriarchal ideal of women distancing themselves from feminist initiatives, Mitchell very explicitly cast herself as a supporter and participant in the event and the Project. Some may fault Mitchell for her lack of objectivity and for giving so much attention to a group she belongs to, but according to feminist principles of validity, she was using a different but legitimate form of objectivity, that is, she gave full disclosure about her involvement with the Project and her role in planning the event. This is much better than other news coverage that pretends to be neutral when, in fact, it is presenting a version of events that is influenced by the reporter and the publication's politics. The amount of space Mitchell devoted to the story, the story's professional but approachable tone, the number of photos and intelligent quotations, the complete lack of delegitimizing frames and the reporter's informed stance on the Project indicate a need for feminist groups to own their own media, whether it be in the form of mass market or independent Do It Yourself (DIY) sources. Increasing the number of political supporters like Mitchell, who are not afraid to explicitly position themselves alongside feminist groups to cover events and align themselves with those initiatives, could lead to more positive media coverage.

WOMEN'S NEWS AND FEMINIST VIEWS: HERIZONS

*[*Herizons *mission is to] empower women: to inspire hope and foster a state of wellness that enriches women's lives: to build awareness of issues as they affect women; to promote the strength, wisdom and creativity of women; to broaden the boundaries of feminine to include building coalitions and support among other marginalized people; to foster peace and ecological awareness; and to expand the influence of feminist principles in the world.* HERIZONS *aims to reflect a feminist philosophy that is diverse, understandable and relevant to women's daily lives.*
— Herizons *Editorial Board*

In its fall 2006 issue, *Herizons* magazine devoted the majority of a page in the "News" section to the Miss G__ Project, mentioning the Read-In but also speaking more broadly of the group's goals and past work. Written by Rachel Thompson, the article connected the work of this group with the historical problem of women's school-based oppression: "Getting a bad deal from high school," she wrote, "is not unfamiliar to those who found it a place where feminism was the f-word" (7). The accompanying photo was of A. Rawlings at the Read-In — a well-known young poet who read from her 2006 collection of poems, *Wide Slumber for Lepidopterists* — rather than any of the steering committee members. This was a first for Project coverage, but members believed that it represented a good shift — rather than the steering committee themselves being the personalized focus of media reporting, the focus was on the event and the event's participants, as well as on the Project's work and goals. The web address for the Project was provided at the end of the article so that readers who wanted more information could get it from Project members themselves. This coverage was

Branding Miss G___

interesting because while it was timed in response to an event, it discussed the goals of the Project to a greater degree than the Read-In and, for a social change group that plans events specifically to gain a media profile for their cause, this was an important accomplishment.

The *Herizons* coverage, though short, was a positive evaluation of the group's mandate and provided informed and relevant information for would-be supporters. I consider this to be among the best coverage the group has seen both for its realistic and positive representation of the group and for its potential for bringing feminist supporters in touch with the Project. While papers such as the *Toronto Star* may attract a greater number of readers, *Herizons* reaches a larger number of feminists who are more likely to provide the kind of strategic political support the group requires.

SHAMELESS MAGAZINE: FOR GIRLS WHO GET IT

Because we learn what it is to be a woman from Seventeen *magazine.*
— Nicole Cohen, "Ruling Class"

In the fall 2006, the Miss G___ Project received coverage in the magazine *Shameless*, which gears itself towards young feminists or, as the editors put it, "girls who get it." *Shameless* editor Nicole Cohen wrote a full-length feature on the Project that focused on the June 6th Read-In. Entitled "Ruling Class," it was relevant, entertaining and informative. What's more, it was fierce. The group was presented as intelligent, strategic and unrepentantly feminist. In fact, the term "feminist," which has elsewhere really been treated as the dreaded "f-word," appeared here in the first sentence. Instead of using the popular delegitimizing frame of underreporting attendance at events in her coverage, Cohen noted that "the turnout [was] higher than the organizers anticipated." She presented the same event in a very different way than the mainstream non-feminist publications the *Toronto Star* and *NOW*. For example, she reported that "one day in early June, women and men (including a few under five years old) spread themselves out on the manicured lawn of Queen's Park." This was a far more positive appraisal than that found in *NOW* where men who were present were portrayed as "supportive boyfriend types" rather than "supporters of the cause." In addition, Cohen's article discussed the goals and philosophy of the Project in ways that mainstream news coverage did not:

> "When you're in school, you're taught about racism, homophobia, sexism and classism separately," says Mohan. "Teaching people about these systems in such a way leads to a fragmented understanding. I learned to look at myself as racialized in one moment and gendered in another, when my reality isn't like that." The women want an intersectional approach to the course, one that recognizes the spaces where oppressions meet and works through holistic understandings of people's social locations. They will not be satisfied with what they call an "add women and stir" approach that would see women-focused topics get a couple of days at the end of a course. "We see this course as a great catalyst for changing the entire education system," Ghabrial says. "We don't see that change coming from sprinkling a few women's names into a course; we want to do it in a much more profound way." (n.p.)

I asked group members how often reporters asked about the philosophy of the group or what would be involved in establishing a women's and gender studies course and the answer was "not that often." Although when the question is asked, members do describe the pluralist focus of the proposed course, happily. Group members believe that many reporters in the mainstream media do not have the grounding in feminist theory or justice education to really understand the intersectionality of oppressions that a women's and gender studies course would address, so often when they do explain what they propose, the coverage instead mentions whatever issue is believed to be plaguing young women at the time, such as self-esteem discourse or raunch culture (see, for example Mills 2006, 25).

Members believe that if more mainstream readers really understood the nature of the proposed course, they may be less likely to support the Project, since the group's goals of exposing and addressing oppression runs contrary to the status quo. The group's goals are clearly "feminist" in nature and, as I have discussed, "feminism" is not supported by much of the mainstream public. The group believes that many people who learn about Miss G__ through the mainstream media see women's studies as an initiative to "Celebrate women!" rather than to combat the intersectionality of gender oppression. It is paradoxical that the group believes it needs positive mainstream media coverage to be successful, while acknowledging that much of the support they can gain from it is from people who misunderstand their goals and might not continue their support if they did understand. The belief that some of the Project's superficial supporters would not continue their support if they had a better understanding of the group's politics has been reinforced by some conservative members leaving because they could not reconcile their personal political beliefs with the pluralist intent of the course (that is, covering issues of race, sexual orientation, disability/ability and so on). Media coverage that emphasizes the transformational nature of a women's studies course is important for accurately spreading the word, and judging by Miss G__'s past coverage, this is delivered by feminist media.

Additionally, feminist coverage has stressed that the work undertaken by the Miss G__ Project is not new but joins a rich tradition of feminists working to open spaces in the realm of education for women's work and women's voices. As Cohen (2006) reported, "Their goal is not a new one. Earlier generations of women have introduced women's studies into high school curricula and struggled to keep it there" (n.p.). As the mainstream media puts so much effort into drawing lines between feminist organizations, pitting the "old" against the "new," this kind of coverage that stresses continuance rather than conflict is invaluable, not just to the groups being discussed but to the wider women's movement. Backlash polarization of the movement has been so successful that many believe that second wave and third wave feminists are diametrically opposed.

Previously, I discussed the media-inspired but publicly accepted popular casting of younger and older feminists as warring mothers and daughters, which contrasts to Robin Morgan's (2003) desire that we "do it as sisters — approaching one another in all our flawed glorious humanity" (576), working together to create cross-generational "feminist diplomacy." This can only be done if the connections linking past, present and future feminism and all that it has accomplished are stressed rather than constantly disrupted. Media coverage that stresses continuity can only lead to greater coalition building between feminist groups.

The *Shameless* coverage marked the first time a feminist or left-leaning news source choreographed photographs of the group. *Herizons* and *The Grapevine* printed candid photos of the Read-In but none that specifically featured the steering committee. The *Shameless* photos also included Jenna Owsianik, who has taken a strong leadership role in the Project. In these photos, the women were wearing the new and improved Miss G__ T-shirts, in darker, richer and less stereotypically feminine colours, like forest green. They were taken at the University of Toronto's historic Hart House and showed Miss G__ members reading and looking mischievous or standing at a podium with scattered papers around them. In every picture, it was clear that they were having fun. They looked smart. They looked like themselves, and they looked like they knew, and loved, what they were doing. The process of taking these pictures was as different for members as the end result:

> *Rawal*: We went to Hart House, the debating room at U of T and the room was very old looking with pictures of the old patriarchs in frames, and there was a throne.
>
> *Ghabrial*: This was way different [than other photos], we were chatting with the photographer and stuff and it was much less choreographed. Usually the photographer has a very specific idea of how they want to use us, like when we did *the London City Life* or the *[London] Free Press* guy who positioned us very exactly, but here the photographer was almost silent, and we decided how we wanted to pose.

Branding Miss G__

Rawal: And they would throw out ideas but it was fun, they seemed to be more honest and understanding that we wanted to play with things, like the old traditional, and then we all had drinks after and chatted and it was fun.

Additionally, in the cartoon depiction of a classroom scene on the cover, *Shameless* portrayed a diverse group of high school age students having a raucous time, which I believe symbolizes students' ability to reclaim their education from patriarchal classroom texts and conventions and create something truly transformative.

IF YOU WANT SOMETHING DONE RIGHT, DO IT YOURSELF

It is about looking at something and saying "I can do that!" rather than waiting for someone to do it for you. It is about taking control away from corporate consumer influence and creating things on your own terms.

— Alex Wrekk, *Stolen Sharpie Revolution*

The kind of coverage the group received from left-leaning and feminist media such as *The Grapevine, Shameless* and *Herizons* is drastically different and better than the mainstream coverage, both in terms of presenting a positive and accurate portrait of the group and its work and in gaining support from the kinds of people most likely to be effective allies in lobbying. Despite the fact that these three sources are all feminist, they each attract a broad audience. *Herizons* is geared mainly to adult feminists, while *Shameless* is geared specifically to teens. *The Grapevine* is distributed only on UWO's campus, which results in its being read widely by professors, staff members and students. Under the editorship of Mitchell and co-editor Fraser Page in 2006–2007, *The Grapevine* gained a reputation for left-wing politics and became specifically sought out by a left-leaning student base. In my mind, this points to an incredible possibility for initiatives like Miss G__ to do the vast majority of its lobbying in alternative media that are more likely to give them positive coverage.

I asked the group to describe the kind of feedback they had received on their mainstream media coverage and I noticed some unsurprising trends, given the frames the media used to delegitimize the Project. Members of the general public who had seen the group in the media, both in the *Toronto Star* and *London City Life*, and had approached them about the articles had no idea what the group stood for, even after seeing them covered in the media. Ghabrial explained,

> My encounters with feedback haven't really been with people who saw us in magazines, except for that one time when people thought we were a band, after we were on the cover of *London City Life* and this guy thought we were in a band and he was like, "So are you going to go on tour?" and it was really funny, like our image had been [girl grouped].

Rawal agreed that she had experienced similar feedback when "once [after the Luncheon] we were at a Starbucks and someone was like, 'I saw you in the [*Toronto Star*]!' and she didn't really know what it was for, but she thought we were pretty glamorous at least." They found that the most informed feedback came after speaking engagements or workshops, in which Project members had the opportunity to display their intelligence, their commitment and their passion for the Project.

This points to several major problems with using the mainstream news as a means of spreading the Project's message. First, the mainstream media used delegitimizing framing techniques which, while subtle, reduced the potential for the group and its activities to be taken seriously. There is a problem when the *Toronto Star* is concerned with the kind of shoes an activist wears (Wells 2005) rather than the serious lack of female presence in education that she is lobbying against. Secondly, because the mainstream media does not take the time to describe the philosophy of the Project, even support that is gained from this kind of coverage is shallow and superficial and is not at all what groups like Miss G__ should be striving to attain. Camauer (2000) discusses that even sympathetic coverage of feminist issues in the mainstream media can "silence [the group or

Branding Miss G___

event's] controversial features" (173). A respondent in Camauer's study reported that "newspapers are not interested in discussing power relations, they want descriptions and smutty details" (178). This agrees with accounts by members of the Miss G__ Project that reporters have "not that often" asked them what their version of a women's studies course entails, leading them to wonder "if it's something that we're trying to filter away from the public perception, or is it something that we're straight up about in interviews and people don't publish it." Thirdly, it has been illustrated that image-based feminist lobbying in the mainstream media is just not that effective. The ways in which feminist stories are presented — as fluff material, with a painfully dumbed-down conversational tone and demeaning or demonizing pictures — means the message is not getting across.

Miss G__'s attempts to disseminate its work in the mainstream media by participating in its capitalist "exchange of women" has not resulted in a public understanding of what the Project actually is and what it actually stands for. As Rebick and Roach (1996) explain, "The media [are] not in the business of doing public relations for social movements" (44), including feminism, and so many feminist groups that rely on the mainstream media to disseminate their message are finding the process to be problematic and ineffective. The Miss G__Project has recently decided to change its media approach quite a bit. The members still believe that in many ways their early image was effective for gaining them support, despite evidence that in fact the support they gained through their mainstream media reports was short-sighted and not in accordance with their actual philosophy. However, as Rawal noted in a 2007 interview, "The flashy days of Miss G__ are over. They served their purpose, and now we're focusing our energy on other things."

The coverage the group received in the feminist and alternative news points to the fact that there are other, more effective options. The group members mentioned that much of the growth, support and financial contributions they have received have come from public-speaking engagements, facilitating high school workshops, word of mouth about the group and staffing tables at school and community events, as well as from their own website, mailing lists and information booklets. It is clear that the group has profited much more from the positive, relevant and informative coverage they have attained in the feminist media, which might not carry the glitz and glamour of a full-colour photo in the *Toronto Star* but does ensure that people who have interest and experience in feminist politics are learning about the group and supporting them in more effective and less superficial ways. It seems clear that media lobbying campaigns for feminist projects, should attempt to gain the attention of feminist and left-wing news sources; it also seems clear that feminist groups should actively promote themselves and spread their own information through the "mouths of babes," so to speak.

Feminists have long understood the value of controlling their own media to ensure a fair portrayal, especially if their goals run contrary to that of the status quo. In fact, the production and distribution of feminist periodicals is older than the feminist movement itself (Steiner 1992). The feminist media "cry out particularly for social change and justice for women. They deal with gender issues buried, ignored or distorted in mainstream media ... [they] are oppositional, alternative, resistant in both product and press" (123). In some ways, the Miss G__ Project has demonstrated comfort with creating its own press releases, information packages and other communications. Project members have demonstrated skill at disseminating information online, following the tradition of young feminists at large. According to the editorial collective at *Briarpatch* (2006), "young feminists ... have turned to electronic organizing, femblogging, zine publication, creative protest and other decentralized and autonomous projects that offer new venues and approaches for challenging patriarchy" (2). Disseminating information in this way allows feminist groups to be completely in control of their message and in choosing the language, images and layout of their communications, rather than relying on hopes that mainstream, or even sympathetic feminist media, will adequately spread their information. Using electronic communications is simple, inexpensive and can reach a wide segment of the population, making it an

Branding Miss G___

incredibly effective means of spreading information. Victoria Bromley and Aalya Ahmad (2006) discuss the ways Miss G___ members have used "old and new feminist methodologies — blogging and internet media, list serv email technologies, sticker campaigns, squats, irony, cheekiness and humour, as well as demonstrations, petitions, postcard campaigns and political lobbying" (68). I would argue that these grassroots, self-controlled means have been far more successful in gaining and keeping support for the Project, as well as keeping supporters abreast of recent developments, current campaigns and future goals.

In February 2008, Miss G___ members began a campaign they called "No More Miss Nice G___," for which they advised supporters to call the Ministry of Education directly and ask when a women's and gender studies course would be on the curriculum, in light of the January 2008 release of the *Final Report on School Safety* from the School Community Safety Advisory Panel (2008) (commonly known as the Falconer Report, after Julian Falconer), which suggests that "gender-based violence, including sexual assault and sexual harassment, is occurring at alarming rates and is largely going unreported" (10–11). The panel found that "all female students are at risk of gender-based violence. However, race, sexuality, disability, class, immigration status and other factors may play a role in producing vulnerabilities to violence" (12). The report gives over 100 recommendations for improving the state of student safety in Toronto's schools, including a focus on gender-based education programs "that examine the root of violence against girls, healthy relationships and equality among marginalized groups," all aspects of the Miss G___ Project's proposed women's studies course. Miss G___ members were notified of the "No More Miss Nice G___" campaign primarily through a Facebook group, and Jenna Owsianik made a YouTube video advertising the campaign in which she role played a phone call to the ministry, providing the minister of education's phone number, all the while appearing fun, young, smart, sassy and well organized. Approaches like this have been far more effective when controlled by the Project itself, or by sympathetic news outlets, than when handed over to the mainstream news.

My suggestion for localizing media campaigning within feminist news sources will likely face charges of impossibility, as the feminist media are considered by the mainstream to be small and homogenous; however, Creedon (1993) explains that the feminist media are as diverse as the movement itself, including feminist co-ops and businesses, women-only and sex-inclusive projects and a wide variety of published communication materials (73). Every women's studies department in every university in the province publishes a magazine, as small as they might be. Additionally, many schools have a Public Interest Research Group (PIRG), which publishes materials that teach area activists how to lobby on a local level. DIY leaflets, copied and distributed by members of the feminist community, have been a consistent feature across the movement, appearing as tracts in the first wave, manifestas in the second and zines in the third. Now, more and more feminist media sources exist online, taking the form of websites, blogs and online periodicals. These allow information to be disseminated widely and quickly, increasing the potential for networking and coalition building.

In Canada, we are lucky to have several good feminist and left-leaning magazines that are good options for Miss G__ to use for spreading information. There is the excellent online feminist journal *Thirdspace*, which frequently publishes articles by and about young feminists. Of course, there are the feminist magazines that have run articles on Miss G__ before, *Shameless* and *Herizons*, and there are the leftist magazines *This*, *Briarpatch*, *Canadian Dimension* and *Maisonneuve* that would all provide an appropriate venue for coverage. The Miss G__ Project was featured in both the fall 2007 and winter 2008 issues of the Canadian Centre for Policy Alternatives' education magazine *Our Schools / Our Selves*. The first of the two articles (both of which were written by myself) detailed the group's 2007 revamping of its mission statement so that it would focus more broadly on equity in education, proposing a women's and gender studies course rather than merely continuing to lobby a seemingly unresponsive government for an official women's studies curriculum (Miller 2007, 90). The second article, "It's Time to Take the Teaching Gender Aptitude Course," was written as a quiz and identified the group specifically as "a grassroots young feminist organization working to combat all forms of oppression in and through education" (Miller 2008, 131). In the winter of 2008, Miss G__ was featured in Toronto's *McClung's* magazine, in an article that discussed the challenges Miss G__ has faced with regards to the government's lack of action. Written by Lora Grady, the article quotes Dr. Rebecca Coulter, an early mentor for the group and long-time activist for equity in education, as saying, "I think there just isn't the political will there to do it, and we get brushed off with the same kinds of arguments that we've been brushed off with for the last 30 years" (n.p.).

Alternative and feminist publications can help the Project build a better, stronger and less superficial base of support. What's more, these media would allow the members to feature their writing skills — rather than their good looks — to further the fun public image they wish to present. As well, the feminist and alternative media would reduce the need for Miss G__ to buy into the neoliberal capitalist "everything is for sale — even us" model of lobbying and instead allow it to focus on strengthening the group's politics. Of course, this does not mean forgetting the mainstream media altogether. Rebick and Roach (1996) argue that "alternatives are important, but they're not a substitute for better coverage in mainstream media" (49). This may be true, but since there is no real way for feminist initiatives such as the Miss G__ Project to ensure that mainstream media coverage will be "better" than what they have achieved so far, it is important for them to focus at least equal effort on getting the word out in alternative ways. Gloria Steinem (2003) warns against "ceding to others control of mainstream media that still elects candidates and frames social policy" (113). It is important to use the mainstream media to spread the word that social movements exist and are working to make significant policy change, and it is incredibly important for feminist groups to continuously question the media, for example, by writing letters to the editors of the dailies. My argument is simply that it is not intelligent to expect the mainstream media to give movements that oppose the status quo the kind of honest and dynamic coverage they both need and deserve. Steinem goes on to ask, "The question isn't: which media to use? The question is: how to use them all?" (114). In order to effectively "use them all," feminists and other activists must understand the kinds of coverage they can expect from different sources and tailor their campaigns to this understanding, while supplementing all press releases with a Project-run information blitz.

The Miss G__ Project may be media savvy, but I think it is clear that in the beginning members underestimated their ability to gain support for the politics of the Project, and as many women do when they doubt their abilities and political power, they worked hard on creating an attractive image rather than on expressing their politics effectively. In fact, the group allowed their politics to be obscured by their appearances. Only around the time of the Read-In did group members begin to feel comfortable enough with their politics to stop focusing on a feminized appearance to suit photo ops in the *Toronto Star* and have the confidence to stand in Queen's Park and chant with Judy Rebick, "What do we want?" "Women's studies!" "When do we want it?" "Now!" It should be the politics of the group and not their favourite footwear that make their goal a viable one. However, if Shdorkoff's concern that they might not have received so much media attention if they had worn track pants or were "dyke looking" is anything to go by, there is the chance that group members continue to believe in some ways that their effectiveness is due to their appearance rather than their politics.

I have discussed that the members of the group display some willingness to publicly compromise their political vision in the mainstream media in order to gain more support. I worry that the kind of mainstream support the group will gain using this kind of strategy will do more harm than good. The Miss G__ Project seeks equity in education. This means something much more than an apolitical "women in history" survey course. Unfortunately, it is that kind of unthreatening non-feminist course that is more likely to be supported by the mainstream public, because that kind of a course doesn't challenge the status quo. This points to the fact that feminism, if it is to be transformational, cannot be "palatable." As the Miss G__ Project purports to seek real educational change, I worry that members will be disturbed by the apolitical "success" their efforts might gain. I worry that a reliance on unthreatening appearances — both physically and politically — may lead to superficial and apolitical support that will lead to the adoption of a substantially different course than the one hoped for. I fear that the course they will lobby into existence will be just the non-feminist "celebration of women's voices" they appear in the public imagination to have been asking for.

Chapter 5

FROM BRANDING TO POLITICAL ACTION

While, in one sense, Miss G. [sic] is narrowly focused on education, in another, it has demonstrated far-reaching possibilities for coalition-building and transformations in Canadian feminist activism.
— Victoria Bromley and Aalya Ahmad, "Wa(i)ving Solidarity"

SINCE ITS INCEPTION, THE MISS G__ PROJECT AND ITS IMAGE have both undergone huge transformations. These changes have made this book as much a review of the growth and development of a lobbying initiative as it has a critique of a cultivated public image. These changes have been incredibly exciting for me, both as a researcher and as a member of Miss G__. In three years, Miss G__'s public image has evolved from a foursome of ostensibly white(ish) and heterosexual(ish) giggling gals with shopping bags in hand and a women's studies course on the brain to a diverse group of women who rely on their strategy and strength, their intelligence and passion to lobby effectively against hatred and misogyny. Of course, these changes are somewhat fluid, and there are times that they have overlapped. The Miss G__ Project has always had a website, found at www.themissgproject.org, and recently launched a Facebook group to keep members and supporters abreast of campaigns and feminist news. Recently, however, it seems that the Project has

Branding Miss G___

begun to heavily lean on these communication tools to spread their information themselves, in their cheeky Miss G__ way.

On March 30, 2007, the UWO's *The Gazette* published its annual April Fools "Spoof" issue, which featured an anonymously penned article called "Labia Majora Carnage," in which a student activist is depicted as being sexually assaulted by London's chief of police while participating in a "Take Back the Nightie *[sic]* March" (6). This story was only one of an entire issue full of misogyny, homophobia and mindless hate literature, which, while not out of the ordinary for *The Gazette*, was rendered all the more problematic by its treatment of rape as a joke and of sexual harassment as an appropriate form of treatment for feminists on campus. Of twenty-two "funny" articles in this issue, fully eleven of them had as their basic message the vilification or sexualization of women or queer people. That this provoked extreme outrage in the campus and wider community is not surprising. However, the amount of attention this atrocity attracted must be attributed in large part to the efforts of Miss G__ members as well as to other equity-concerned campus groups who put sleeping and eating, along with their own scholarly and professional lives and leisure, on the backburner to campaign against such blatant sexual harassment in student publications.

Members of the Miss G__ Project initiated a strong letter writing campaign, advising students, staff, faculty, alumni, parents and community members to write their own letters of outrage to the university's administration, *The Gazette* office, the University Student Council (USC) president and campus equity services. Simultaneously, Miss G__ ran an information blitz, sending letters and press releases to every news outlet and feminist blog, MPP and MP, feminist and GLBT activist, women's group and sexual assault centre they could think of. As a participant in this blitz, I know that every member of the Project at a local level devoted all of her time and energy to spreading information, discussing the issue with students, doing interviews in local and national news, attending meetings and working hard to ensure that this kind of article could never again make it into UWO's campus papers. Many people believed that this article reflected a broader "chilly climate" for women at UWO, which had been originally documented when UWO Women's Caucus members Roma Harris, Connie Backhouse, Gill Mitchell and Alison Wylie released their "Chilly Climate Report" that highlighted employment inequity with regards to faculty women in 1989.

The administration was unwilling or unable to address this issue with a suitable and legitimate answer in the days after the article ran, so student groups such as the Miss G__ Project carried the momentum of frustration and anger and turned it into a vehicle for campaigning harder and smarter than they had before. The campaign was heavily organized by Miss G__ member Laurel Mitchell, who wrote press releases, gave interviews, sent letters, worked her phone tree and set up a Facebook site. The site allowed Miss G__ to spread information about the issue, gave students a forum where they could express their fears and concerns, and provided quick access to addresses and telephone numbers of everyone at the university whose job it was to ensure that articles like this were never to happen in the first place. The Facebook group attracted members in the thousands, and many people even outside of the UWO community wrote in and expressed their disgust at *The Gazette*. Feminist blogs from across North America discussed the issue and the role of Miss G__ in raising awareness and demanding restitution. During gatherings such as the UWO Town Hall meeting, which was held to allow community members the opportunity to speak publicly about their personal connection to the issue and which attracted political and community figures from London's broader population, Miss G__ members set up a blog and live-cast the event for people who couldn't be there. There was also a YouTube video produced by Jenna Owsianik and others entitled "University of Western Rapists Ontario" (which can be seen at www.youtube.com/watch?v=WMeZDVDYKjA).

In the end, what Miss G__ members wanted from the university and *The Gazette* was a formal apology and guarantees that accountability measures would be taken by both the paper and the administration to ensure that this kind of hate speech would not be repeated and, that if it was, students would have a process of

Branding Miss G__

effectively voicing their concerns and having those concerns heard. Many of these goals have been achieved. Eventually, official apologies, some of which even seemed legitimate, were released by Paul Davenport, president of the university; Ian Van Den Hurk, *The Gazette*'s editor-in-chief; and Fab Dolan, president of the University Student's Council (USC). UWO's administration has changed its hands-off policy with regards to *The Gazette* content. The USC response has been to institute "a series of reforms for the paper including the development of a journalistic code of ethics, better training for editors, including sensitivity and ethics sessions, and a complaints process that would allow students to initiate a petition to remove an editor from office" (Klanac 2007, n.p.). During this campaign, Project members really proved their passion for and commitment to equity in education for female and queer students and set themselves apart as well-organized leaders opposing campus hatred.

I have never been as proud of my membership in the Miss G__ Project as I was during those two weeks when I could work politically with my friends in this group to make a public statement against violence against women on campus. It would be egotistical and false of me to attribute the changes in Miss G__'s lobbying and campaigning style to myself and/or the influence of this book; however, many of my suggestions for better practice were adopted and used in this campaign, such as letting strong politics and intelligence overshadow good looks and great shoes, instead of the other way around. While Miss G__ members played a key role in opposing hate speech during this campaign, not one photograph of them appeared in any news source, online or in print. Members of the Project spoke to CBC Radio, CHRW campus radio's *Broadly Speaking* program, *Shameless* and the *Toronto Star*. In the *Star*'s article written by Louise Brown (2007), Brown quoted Project member Laurel Mitchell as saying that "to use the image of rape to 'teach a woman a lesson' is not funny; it's a violent, personal attack that has no business in a student publication" (12). This is a far cry from the giggling girl in a short skirt image reported by Brown following the "New Girls' Club Luncheon," just a year earlier. The absence of photographs worked to the Project's benefit, because it allowed them to be serious and maintain a legitimacy and diversity of member's voices that have not always been present in its lobbying efforts. Of course, Miss G__ members maintained a sense of their fun and young image in their written communications by keeping their sense of humour intact. But they didn't allow their own cuteness or cleverness to overshadow the fact that there was a massive problem that needed to be addressed and resolved.

Although I had not considered suggesting that this group alter its mandate in any way, I believe now that the strength of Miss G__ lies in its ability to organize campaigns and broadcast issues. While the goal of creating and instituting a women's and gender studies course continues to be the group's main professed goal, I believe that this Project would serve well as a feminist watch dog organization, using its formidable contact list, passion and intelligence to help facilitate campaigns against educational inequity. Members of the Miss G__ Project are excellent at gaining public attention. They work their activist phone tree in ways that should make their second wave feminist role models proud. Of course, the group needs to work on being less of a "media darling" than they have tended to be, focusing less on their own cuteness in ways that can detract attention from the issues they attempt to address (and yes, as a Project member myself, I have also been guilty of this activist self-love). I believe Miss G__ also has a great potential role in helping teachers gather and use feminist materials, to connect with other activist teachers and to feel that they have the support needed to integrate feminism at a grassroots classroom level.

My original suggestion was that the group focus on spreading their message more centrally through the feminist and sympathetic media, which would allow them to maintain a purity of vision, involving critiques of gender, race, class and sexuality power struggles, which they did not see as possible when working within the popular media. While I still believe that within feminist lobbying better information dissemination occurs in sympathetic

Branding Miss G___

rather than popular media, and that cutting away at feminist politics to increase palatability is a huge mistake (even if you plan to pull "the old bait and switch" after obtaining support), the two weeks following *The Gazette* incident have shown me that Miss G___ can, in fact, work within the popular media to gain support for feminist causes without "selling out," as is my fear, and without alienating the audience, as is theirs. Of course, their success in appearing professional and knowledgeable in the mainstream media was no substitute for the incredible amount of information dissemination they did themselves, setting up an open group on Facebook, using mass emails, phone calls and a feminist blog, which allowed them to keep the interested public up to date in real time.

During this campaign, group members allowed themselves to slip to the background, allowing the issue to take the limelight. Instead of focusing on which bag to bring to the protest, they focused on getting as many people as possible to attend a Town Hall meeting on the issue, to write letters in protest and call the administration, and they didn't worry whether USC members would think they were lesbians or brand them as "angry." In this protest, they displayed a confidence that was new to the group, perhaps because they thought the issue was one which deserved and would gain more support than their original goal of a women's and gender studies course, or perhaps because they were beginning to feel more secure in their role and strength as organizers. I like to believe it was the latter, and that the group will continue to organize in this manner: focusing on the issues; seeking out coalitions with other community groups, whether or not they are fashionable; speaking out from a diversity of voices rather than emphasizing homogeneity, appealing to a more diverse spectrum; and organizing with gender justice, rather than gender-complimentary appearance in mind.

In an interview in December 2007, Rawal told me that she believes that, in the beginning, it was important for Miss G___ to appear palatable and less political than it really was to gain support and attention, and now that they have that attention, they can afford to appear more the way they actually are and say more of what they actually mean. In 2008, the Project members launched their Valentine's Day campaign under the name of "No More Miss Nice G__!" The goal was to flood the phone lines of then minister of education Kathleen Wynne all day on Valentine's Day with individuals calling to ask when she planned to honour her commitment to put a women's and gender studies course in the high school curriculum. Project member Jenna Owsianik created an amazing information video for this event, which I believe captured the perfect blend of Miss G__'s young and fun image while still showing that Miss G__ members are smart, strategic and well organized. (See the appendix for a complete script of the video.) This video, which has been viewed thousands of times on YouTube (see http://soapboxspinster.blogspot.com/2008/02/no-more-miss-nice-g.html), begins with Owsianik waiting by the phone:

> Have you ever met someone really great, and you just had this awesome connection, and you couldn't believe they were saying all the right things at all the right times, and you think 'this is it!' Everything is going sooo good. They promise you that they're going to be there, and you believe them. Sometimes things start to get a little rough at the office. Things start picking up and they get busy, and you think that's life, it happens, so you think, alright, I'll just wait a little bit. They said they're going to call, why would they say they were going to call and then not call?

A few minutes into the video, we learn that the call Owsianik is awaiting isn't from her boyfriend or girlfriend, but rather from the minister of education. Eventually, Owsianik decides that the minister is "never going to call" and takes matters into her own hands, "And that's why it's no more Miss Nice G__!" The screen cuts to a pink-screened image of the Miss G__ logo with the name of the campaign. Owsianik goes on to role play a possible phone call between a Project supporter and Kathleen Wynne's assistant (playing both roles herself). She tells callers to be "polite but firm," to mention the Falconer Report's belief that equity in education programming is an effective preventative measure in stopping school violence against women, and to include an anecdote from their personal experience.

Branding Miss G__

The video is fun and funny, and Owsianik looks really good in it. She's wearing a pink striped shirt and has a cute haircut. But no reasonable person watching the video is going to focus on that. Her good looks take a very definite backseat to her political message. This should be the kind of thing the Miss G__ Project strives for in all of their future campaigns — combining their politics with their fun in such a way that the politics come first.

When I began my research for this book, I was much less critical of the cultivated public image of Miss G__, as were other Project members. We were all having a lot of fun, we enjoyed being photographed for the *Toronto Star* and being "fashion feminists" and theory-loving girls who went on "latte promenades" and danced the revolution Tuesday nights. I envisioned this work to be a far more glowing appraisal of the Project, the third wave and especially "girlie" feminism. But as I read more and more feminist theory from across and within the waves, and participated in the evolving Miss G__ Project, my understanding of the role of image in feminist lobbying was drastically altered (although my love of lattes and dancing was not). That has made writing this book a bit more difficult. Every time I thought I had come close to finishing, I stumbled upon some new information or the Project began a new campaign and my ground became shaky. This is the problem with studying a group in "real time," and at certain points I wished I were writing this five years from now, when I could look back with more history between us, and consequently, more certainty of strategic outcomes. What I can say unequivocally is that the work of this Project joins the efforts of many feminists who came before us and opened up much-needed critical spaces for women across the education system. I'm proud to have been able to help capture a small piece of their history in the making of Miss G__, adding to the small canon of feminist writing about the women's movement in Canada and, particularly, about the work of young women in it.

While the members of the Miss G__ Project fit the established mould of a third wave feminist initiative in many ways, including their age, their dexterity in using technology and their emphasis on a "girlie" image for lobbying purposes, in several ways they break away from third wave feminist patterns. First, the group focuses on organizing and working politically as a collective, both in and of itself and alongside other groups to achieve its goals. Second, although the Project doesn't have a strict, top-down hierarchical organization, in many ways it has an established leadership base. Ghabrial, Mohan, Rawal and Shdorkoff, as well as Laurel Mitchell and Jenna Owsianik, really seem to be at the helm for most of the provincial lobbying and campaigning. While the group is fluid in the sense that anyone can step up and initiate a campaign, most large-scale endeavours are undertaken by this key group. Third, Project members seek coalition with more experienced feminists, community members and teachers, and for the most part, honour and respect their feminist foremothers. Fourth, while the group does engage with cultural production and commodification, they bring their feminism to life in the public and political realms as well. I believe that the way Miss G__ has acquiesced with the third wave tradition are the areas with which they have difficulty, for example, their initially uncritical use of "girlie" feminism, which interrupts the potential for working-class, poor and gender-non-conforming people to participate. The project's "dutiful daughter" relationship with ministry of education officials and its participation in a neo-liberal capitalist "everything is for sale – even feminism" discourse is troublesome if the course they envision is truly transformational, which it is.

Over the course of writing this book, I've been asked more times than I can count whether members of Miss G__ are going to be "mad at me" for my criticisms. At our December 2007 interview, we discussed the issue that no one seems to believe that feminists within groups can be critical of our own practices. Ghabrial pointed out that critiques from inside can be really useful, "We want to own our own critiques. I mean, the way we do it, sitting down and talking it through, then writing and emailing about it, it's strategic." Rawal agrees, "It's when it happens behind your back that it sucks. And it's not productive." None of the criticisms present in this book

Branding Miss G__

are new to members of the Project, who have spent hours discussing these issues at parties, over breakfast, at planning meetings, the pub, through text messages, Gmail chat and everywhere in between. My belief that the Project, if it is to be successful the way I know it wants to be successful, needs to facilitate a greater consistency between their image and their goals has been a long-standing discussion within the group at the same time as it has been the subject of this book. And while we at Miss G__ agree that it might help sell more copies to have a (fake) public feud about it, we're really over feminist drama. We'd prefer to work together to facilitate change in our own organizations, in schools and in broader society.

After years of playing the "girl," the time has come for Miss G__ to come of age, to get "critical and strategic" (Rebick & Roach 1996, 89), and for Project members to be seen as a force to be reckoned with, as a serious feminist endeavour. The challenge is to undo some of the pink and lavender girlie-girl damage they did while seeking initial approval and support. bell hooks (1992) wrote in *Black Looks: Race and Representation,* "While it is crucial that women come to voice in a patriarchal society that socializes us to repress and contain, it is also crucial what we say, how we say it and what our politics are" (80). I believe that Miss G__ has, at this time, come to voice, and it is time for group members to continue in the work they've been doing of late to more truly align their words and actions with their politics. It is time for Miss G__ to go forward with their current mandate to "combat all forms of oppression in and through education" (Miss G__ Project 2007a, n.p.), fulfilling its potential to be a real transformational feminist presence in Ontario's education system, whether it be through the development and institutionalization of a women's and gender studies course, the facilitation of consciousness-raising high school workshops, as an educational watchdog organization, by using their networking skills to bring feminist educators together or through the creation of curriculum and policy resources.

Miss G__ members have proven themselves able to do all of these things. Now the time has come for the group to continue strengthening its political presence and strategy, to put its politics where its practice is and to ensure a more consistent link between the two. Maintaining a marriage between fun and lobbying is integral. That the members of Miss G__ truly enjoy their work is an exciting and valuable resource. I think that going forward with the awareness the members now have, they could easily and more rigorously plan events like the Luncheon and the Read-In not only to be fun and carry the distinct Miss G__ flavour but also to deliver their political goals and philosophy with intelligence and confidence. The members are ready to focus less on getting coverage in the mainstream media and facilitating one-sidedly good relationships with politicians in the media and more on running their own press through blogs and the feminist and leftist news, while building relationships with other feminist groups whose support will help Miss G__ apply political pressure and get what's really coming to them. This is the approach that will help reduce the need for Miss G__ to compromise its vision and pander to conservatives and non-feminists whose superficial support could never truly help the group succeed.

APPENDIX

NO MORE MISS NICE G__!
Valentine's Day Phone-In Video,
February 14, 2008

Written & Produced by Jenna Owsianik
* Reprinted here with the permission of the author.

[Screen opens with a headshot of Jenna, talking to the audience.]

JENNA: Have you ever met someone really great? And you just had this awesome connection? And you couldn't believe that they were saying all the right things at all the right times? And you finally think to yourself that, I mean, this is it! Everything is going so good. They promise you that they're going to be there, and you believe them.

Branding Miss G___

Sometimes things start to get a little rough at the office, things start picking up and they get busy and you know that's life, it happens. So I think, alright I'll just, I'll just wait a little bit. They said that they were going to call. Why would someone say that they're gonna to call and just not call?

Voice over: A few weeks pass by and you still haven't heard from them. It's like your doctor is the only one that wants to contact you.

[The telephone rings.]

JENNA: Hello? I have vaginitis? What's that?

[Subtitle across the screen:] True story.

Voice over: Or from someone else you're just not expecting.

[The telephone rings.]

JENNA *(in an impatient voice)*: What do you want Sheetal?

SHEETAL: Ughh.

APPENDIX ·

JENNA: Then it hits you. It probably should've a really long time ago. But, they're not gonna call. They're probably never gonna call. And that's why it's No More Miss Nice G__!

[Slides enter with a popular song playing.]

[slide 1:] This February 14, 2008 …

[slide 2:] rekindle that old flame

[slide 3:] call your mom, your lover …

[slide 4:] and the Ministry of Education

[slide 5:] because it is …

[slide 6:] NO MORE MISS NICE G__!!

[Music and slides end; back to Jenna.]

Branding Miss G___

JENNA: On February 14th we're asking all Miss G__ supporters to call the Minister of Education, Kathleen Wynne, at the phone number I'm going to leave in the info box of this video until the campaign is over.

Calling this number will take you to the Minister's voice mail or to her personal assistant. If you have any problems please let us know. You shouldn't get to a message board with a list of numeric options, but if something happens just remember: Minister of Education, Kathleen Wynne!

[Subtitle across the screen:] I want to talk to the Minister of Education, Kathleen Wynne!

JENNA: OKAY, so I'm dialing now and I'm getting a little nervous but that's OKAY 'cause we're all going to remember that we're really fabulous, we're really intelligent, and we have something important to say!

[Jenna dials the phone; we hear ringing.]
[Screen switches from Jenna's headshot to Jenna sitting at a desk, in her role as the receptionist.]

APPENDIX ·

RECEPTIONIST: Hello, Minister of Education's office. How may I help you?

JENNA *(to receptionist)*: Hi!

(Aside to audience) Make sure to state your name and where you are from in Ontario. If you are not currently residing in the province indicate what high school you attended.

(To receptionist) My name is Jenna Owsianik and I'm from Toronto, Ontario, and I am calling for the Minister of Education Kathleen Wynne. I really want to find out when it is exactly that she will be honouring her commitment to get a Women's and Gender Studies course added into the Ontario Secondary School Curriculum?

RECEPTIONIST: Well, this issue is on our list of things to do and we will be having a meeting in the future with the Miss G__ Project regarding a possible Women's and Gender Studies course.

[Subtitle across the screen:] Huh? possible?????

Branding Miss G___

JENNA *(to receptionist):* Thank you very much for the information. However, what we're not seeing is any action.

RECEPTIONIST: Well, it's been very good to hear from you, I'll pass that message along.

JENNA *(to receptionist)*: Wait! I have something else to say.

[Subtitle across the screen:] What is your experience?

JENNA *(to receptionist):* When I was in high school I was sexually harassed a few times, and I remember one time in a class I was touched inappropriately by a male student. The teacher saw and the students saw, yet the lesson just kept on going as if nothing happened, sending the message that this is okay.

[Subtitle across the screen:] Falconer Report. Sometimes I pronounce things funny.

JENNA *(to receptionist)*: The release of the *Facloner* Report in January shows that my experience is far from unique and that sexual assault and sexual harassment within high schools are far too common. Including a Women's and Gender studies course into high schools is an extremely important measure in preventing sexual harassment and assault within high schools and in larger society because we can analyze gender and really validate girls' experiences.

RECEPTIONIST: Good on you for calling and expressing your opinion. As a citizen, it is our job to listen to you!

JENNA: Great, thank you very much for your time. I will be in contact with The Miss G__ Project and I'll be following how this progresses.

[Subtitle across the screen:] HOLD THEM ACCOUNTABLE!!

APPENDIX·

JENNA *(to audience):* If you have trouble getting though the first time, why not call back later?

That assistant was pretty great, she might not say that last bit, but it's true. You shouldn't be intimidated.

If you're feeling technologically savvy we encourage you to videotape yourself when you call the Minister of Education and to post it as a video response on Youtube.

[Subtitle across the screen:] Kudos to Kay!

While you're being polite, yet firm, perhaps listening to a little bit of political sweet talk, I want you to remember one thing.

[Slides enter with a popular song playing.]

[slide 1]: NO MORE MISS NICE G___!!

[slide 2]: We are tired of waiting…

Branding Miss G

[slide 3]: WOMEN'S AND GENDER STUDIES

[slide 4]: SOCK IT TO ME!

[slide 5]: www.themissgproject.org

[slide 6]: themissgproject@gmail.com

....

[Music and video ends.]

REFERENCES

Adams, M.L. (1999). *The Trouble with Normal: Postwar Youth and the Making of Heterosexuality.* Toronto: University of Toronto Press.

Ashley, L., and B. Olson. (1998). "Constructing Reality: Print Media's Framing of the Women's Movement, 1966 to 1986." *Journalism and Mass Communication Quarterly* 75: 263–277.

Bailey, C. (1997). "Making Waves and Drawing Lines: The Politics of Defining the Vicissitudes of Feminism." *Hypatia* 12, no. 3: 17–28.

—. (2002). "Unpacking the Mother/Daughter Baggage: Reassessing Second and Third Wave Tensions." *Women's Studies Quarterly* 3, no. 4: 138–154.

Barker-Plummer, B. (1995). "News as a Political Resource: Media Strategies and Political Identity in the U.S. Men's Movement, 1966–1975." *Critical Studies in Mass Communication* 12: 306–324.

Barnard, M. (2002). *Fashion as Communication.* 2nd ed. London: Routledge.

Bartky, S.L. (1997). "Foucault, Femininity, and the Modernization of Patriarchal Power." In K. Conboy, N. Medina and S. Stanbury, eds., *Writing on the Body: Female Embodiment and Feminist Theory*, 129–154. New York: Columbia University Press.

Baumgardner, J. (2007). *Look Both Ways: Bisexual Politics.* New York: Farrar, Straus and Giroux.

Baumgardner, J., and A. Richards. (2000). *Manifesta: Young Women, Feminism and the Future.* New York: Farrar, Straus and Giroux.

Beach, D. (2003). "A Problem of Validity in Educational Research." *Qualitative Inquiry* 9: 859–873.

Bhanavi, K. (2002). "Tracing the Contours: Feminist Research and Feminist Objectivity." In S.N. Hesse-Biber and M.L. Yaiser, eds., *Feminist Perspectives of Social Research,* 65–77. New York: Oxford University Press.

Bourdieu, P. (1997). "The Forms of Capital." In A.H. Halsey et al., eds., *Education: Culture, Economy and Society,* 47–58. New York: Oxford University Press.

Bordo, S. (1997). "The Body and the Reproduction of Femininity." In K. Convoy, N. Medina and S. Stanbury, eds., *Writing on the Body: Female Embodiment and*

Feminist Theory, 80–112. New York: Columbia University Press.

Briarpatch Editorial Collective. (2006). "*Maclean's* and the War on Feminism." *Briarpatch* 35, no. 2: 2.

Briskin, L. (1991). "Feminist Practice: A New Approach to Evaluating Feminist Strategy." In J.D. Wine and J.L. Ristock, eds., *Women and Social Change: Feminist Activism in Canada*, 24–41. Toronto: James Lorimer.

Bromley, V., and A. Ahmad. (2006). "Wa(i)ving Solidarity: Feminist Activists Confronting Backlash." *Canadian Woman Studies/les cahiers de la femme* 25, nos. 3, 4: 61–71.

Bronstein, C. (2005). "Representing the Third Wave: Mainstream Print Media Framing of a New Feminist Movement." *Journalism and Mass Communication Quarterly* 82: 783–803.

Brown, L. (2006, March 30). "Young Feminists on a Mission; Lobby Queen's Park for Women's Studies Course in High School: Bold Group from Western Makes Point with Old Boys Spoof." *Toronto Star*, A18. Retrieved 20 January 2007 from Proquest Canadian Newsstand, available online from https://rsvpn.ubc.ca/http/proquest.umi.com.

—. (2007, April 11). "Spoof of Campus Feminist 'Appalling'; Campus Women's Groups Demand Retraction as Article in Western Ontario Student Paper Blasted." *Toronto Star*, A18. Retrieved 20 April 2007 from Proquest Canadian Newsstand, available online at https://rsvpn.ubc.ca/http/proquest.umi.com.

Bulbeck, C. (2005). "'Women Are Exploited Way Too Often': Feminist Rhetorics at the End of Equality." *Australian Feminist Studies* 20, no. 46: 65–76.

Bullock, H.E., and J.L. Fernald. (2003). "'Feminism Lite?' Feminist Identification, Speaker Appearance, and Perceptions of Feminist and Antifeminist Messengers." *Psychology of Women Quarterly* 27: 291–299.

Buszek, M.E. (July, 2001). "'Oh! Dogma (up yours!)': Surfing the Third Wave." *Thirdspace*. Retrieved 22 July 2006 from http://thirdspace.ca/articles/buszke.htm.

Camauer, L. (2000). "Women's Movements, Public Spheres and the Media: A Research Strategy for Studying Women's Movements' Publicist Practices." In A. Sreberny and L. van Zoonen, eds., *Gender, Politics and Communication*, 161–183. Cresskill, NJ: Hampton.

Chaiken, I. (Writer), and Troche, R. (Director). 2005. "Labia Majora." Episode 1, Season 3, *The L Word* [television]. Los Angeles: Showtime.

Clarke, E.H. (1873). *Sex in Education, or, A Fair Chance for the Girls*. N.p.: n.p.

Cho, M. (2006). "Foreword." In L. Jervis and A. Zeisler, eds., *Bitchfest: Ten Years of Cultural Criticism from the Pages of Bitch Magazine*, xv–xvii. New York: Farrar, Straus and Giroux.

Cohen, N. (2006, Fall). "Ruling Class." *Shameless*. Retrieved 2 February 2007 from

REFERENCES ·

wwww.shamelessmag.com/issues/fall2006/missg/1/.

Costain, A.N., R. Braunstein, and H. Berggen. (1997). "Framing the Women's Movements." In P. Norris, ed., *Women, Media and Politics*, 205–220. Cambridge: University of Oxford Press.

Craig, J. (2006). "I Can't Believe It's Not Feminism: On the Feminists Who Aren't." In L. Jervis and A. Zeisler, eds., *Bitchfest: Ten Years of Cultural Criticism from the Pages of Bitch Magazine*, 116–124. New York: Farrar, Straus and Giroux.

Crane, D. (2000). *Fashion and Its Social Agendas: Class, Gender and Identity in Clothing*. Chicago: University of Chicago Press.

Creedon, P.J. (1993). "Framing Feminism: A Feminist Primer for the Mass Media." *Media Studies Journal* 7, nos. 1, 2: 68–81.

Crosbie, L. (1997). "Introduction." In L. Crosbie, ed., *Click: Becoming Feminists*, 2–5. Toronto: Macfarlane Walter and Ross.

Delombard, J. (2001). "Feminism." In R. Walker, ed., *To Be Real: Telling the Truth and Changing the Face of Feminism*, 21–34. New York: Anchor.

Detloff, M. (1997). "Mean Spirits: The Politics of Contempt between Feminist Generations." *Hypatia* 12: 76–99.

Dent, G. (1995). "Missionary Position." In R. Walker, ed., *To Be Real: Telling the Truth and Changing the Face of Feminism*, 61–75. New York: Anchor.

Dicker, R., and A. Piepmeier. (2003). "Introduction." In R. Dicker and A. Piepmeier, eds., *Catching a Wave: Reclaiming Feminism for the Twenty-first Century*, 3–8. Boston: Northeastern University Press.

DiFranco, Ani. (2007). *Verses*. New York: Seven Stories.

Douglas, S.J. (1995). *Where the Girls Are: Growing Up Female with the Mass Media*. New York: Three Rivers.

Dow, B.J. (1996). *Prime-Time Feminism: Television, Media Culture, and the Women's Movement Since 1970*. Philadelphia: University of Pennsylvania Press.

—. (2003). "Feminism, Miss America and Media Mythology." *Rhetoric and Public Affairs* 6, no. 1: 127–149.

Dubinski, K. (2005, November 24). "Gender Agenda Pushed." *London Free Press*, C6.

Elm, D. (1997). "Sisters Are Doing It to Themselves." In D. Looser and E.A. Kaplan, eds., *Generations: Academic Feminists in Dialogue*, 55–68. Minneapolis: University of Minnesota Press.

Entwistle, J. (2000). *The Fashioned Body: Fashion, Dress and Modern Social Theory*. Cambridge: Polity Press.

Erdman Farrell, A. (1995). "Feminism and the Media: Introduction." *Signs* 20, no. 3: 642–645.

Evans, C., and M. Thornton. (1991). "Fashion, Representation, Femininity."

Feminist Review 38: 48–66.

Faludi, S. (1991). *Backlash: The Undeclared War against American Women.* New York: Crown.

Findlen, B. (2001). "Foreword." In B. Findlen, ed., *Listen Up! Voices from the Next Feminist Generation,* xiii–xvii. Seattle: Seal Press.

Fine, M. (1992). "Passions, Politics and Power: Feminist Research Possibilities." In M. Fine, ed., *Disruptive Voices: The Possibilities of Feminist Research,* 205–232. Ann Arbour: University of Michigan Press.

Freeman, B.M. (2001). *The Satellite Sex: The Media and Women's Issues in English Canada 1966-1971.* Waterloo, ON: Wilfrid Laurier University Press.

Fudge, R. (2006). "Celebrity Jeopardy: The Perils of Feminist Fame." In L. Jervis and A. Zeisler, eds., *Bitchfest: Ten Years of Cultural Criticism from the Pages of Bitch Magazine,* 125–133. New York: Farrar, Straus and Giroux.

Gabriel, J. (1998). *Whitewash: Racialized Politics and the Media.* London: Routledge.

Garrison, E.K. (2000). "U.S. Feminism — Grrrl Style! Youth (Sub)cultures and the Technologics of the Third Wave." *Feminist Studies* 26, no. 1: 141–170.

Gibson, P.C. (2000). "Redressing the Balance: Patriarchy, Postmodernism and Feminism." In S. Bruzzi and P.C. Gibson, eds., *Fashion Cultures: Theories, Explorations and Analysis,* 349–362. New York: Routledge.

Gillis, S., and Munford, R. (2004). "Genealogies and Generations: The Politics and Praxis of Third Wave Activism." *Women's History Review* 13, no. 2: 165–182.

Gitlin, T. (1980). *The Whole World Is Watching: Mass Media and the Making and Unmaking of the New Left.* Berkeley: University of California Press.

Grady, L. (2008). "Miss Educated." *McClung's.* Retrieved 25 January 2008 from www.mcclungs.ca/w2008/16.htm.

Gray, J.M. (2001). "Striking Social Dramas, Image Events, and Meme Warfare: Performance and Social Activism — Past, Present, and Future." *Text and Performance Quarterly* 21, no. 1, 64–75.

Guerilla Girls. (2001). *The Birth of Feminism.* Retrieved 14 March 2007 from http://www.guerrillagirls.com/posters/birthcolor.shtml.

Hamilton, R. (2005). *Gendering the Vertical Mosaic: Feminist Perspectives on Canadian Society.* 2nd ed. Toronto: Prentice Hall.

Hanna, K. (2003). "Gen X Survivor: From Riot Grrrl Rock Star to Feminist Activist." In R. Morgan, ed., *Sisterhood Is Forever: The Women's Anthology for a New Millennium,* 131–137. New York: Washington Square.

Hao, R. (2006). "And Now a Word from Our Sponsors: Feminism for Sale." In L. Jervis and A. Zeisler, eds., *Bitchfest: Ten Years of Cultural Criticism from the Pages of Bitch Magazine,* 111–115. New York: Farrar Straus and Giroux.

Henry, A. (2004). *Not My Mother's Sister: Generational Conflict and Third-Wave*

REFERENCES ·

Feminism. Bloomington: Indiana University Press.

Herizons Editorial Board. (2007, winter). "Mission Statement." *Herizons.*

Hernandez, D., and B. Rehman, eds. (2002). *Colonize This! Young Women of Color on Today's Feminism.* New York: Seal Press.

Hesse-Biber, S.N., and D. Leckenby. (2002). "How Feminists Do Social Research." In S.N. Hesse-Biber and M.L. Yaiser, eds., *Feminist Perspectives of Social Research,* 209–226. New York: Oxford University Press.

Hesse-Biber, S.N., P. Leavy, and M.L. Yaiser. (2002). "Feminist Approaches to Research as a Process: Reconceptualizing Epistemology, Methodology and Method." In S.N. Hesse-Biber and M.L. Yaiser, eds., *Feminist Perspectives of Social Research,* 3–26. New York: Oxford University Press.

Heywood, L., and J. Drake. (1997a). "Introduction." In L. Heywood and J. Drake, eds., *Third Wave Agenda: Being Feminist, Doing Feminism,* 1–20. Minneapolis: University of Minnesota Press.

—. (1997b). "We Learn America like a Script: Activism in the Third Wave; Or, Enough Phantoms of Nothing." In L. Heywood and J. Drake, eds., *Third Wave Agenda: Being Feminist, Doing Feminism,* 40–54. Minneapolis: University of Minnesota Press.

Hinds, H., and J. Stacey. (2001). "Imaging Feminism, Imaging Femininity: The Bra Burner, Diana and the Woman Who Kills." *Feminist Media Studies* 1, no. 2: 153–178.

Hogeland, L.M. (2001). "Against Generational Thinking, or, Some Things that 'Third Wave' Feminism Isn't." *Women's Studies in Communication* 24, no. 1: 107–121.

Hollows, J. (2000). *Feminism, Femininity and Popular Culture.* Manchester: Manchester University Press.

hooks, b. (1984). *Feminist theory: From Margin to Center.* Boston: South End Press.

—. (1992). *Black Looks: Race and Representation.* Toronto: Between the Lines.

—. (1994). *Teaching to Transgress: Education as the Practice of Freedom*: London: Routledge.

—. (1995). "Beauty Laid Bare: Aesthetics in the Ordinary." In R. Walker, ed., *To Be Real: Telling the Truth and Changing the Face of Feminism,* 157–166. New York: Anchor.

—. (2000). *Feminism Is for Everybody: Passionate Politics.* London: Pluto.

Huddy, L. (1997). "Feminists and Feminism in the News." In P. Norris ed., *Women, Media and Politics,* 183–204. Cambridge: University of Oxford Press.

—. (1998). "The Social Nature of Political Identity: Feminist Image and Feminist Identity." Paper presented at the meeting of the American Political Science Association, Boston, MA. Retrieved 23 February 2007 from

Branding Miss G___

http://scholar.google.com/scholar?hl+en&lr=&q+cache:5-aAwBK1vTkJ:ms.cc. sunysb.edu/-lhuddy/huddy98.pdf+huddy+political+identification.

Hurdis, R. (2002). "Heartbroken: Women of Color Feminism and the Third Wave." In D. Hernandez and B. Rehman, eds., *Colonize This! Young Women of Color on Today's Feminism*, 279–294. New York: Seal Press.

Hutcheon, L. (2002). *The Politics of Postmodernism.* 2nd ed. London: Routledge.

Jacob, K., and A.C. Licona. (2005). "Writing the Waves: A Dialogue on the Tools, Tactics and Tensions of Feminism and Feminist Practices Over Time and Place." *NWSA Journal* 17, no. 1: 197–205.

Jervis, L. (2005a). "The End of Feminism's Third Wave." *Ms.* 14, no. 4: 56–58.

—. (2005b, September 15). "If Women Ruled the World, Nothing Would Be Different." *LiP Magazine.* Retrieved 20 September 2006 from http://lipmagazine.org/articles/feajervis_femminsm_p.htm.

—. (2006). "Foreword: Goodbye to Feminism's Generational Divide." In M. Berger, ed., *We Don't Need Another Wave: Dispatches from the Next Generation of Feminists*, 13–17. Emeryville, CA: Seal Press.

Jervis, L., and A. Zeisler. (2006). "The F Word." In L. Jervis and A. Zeisler, eds., *Bitchfest: Ten Years of Cultural Criticism from the Pages of Bitch Magazine*, 106–110. New York: Farrar, Straus and Giroux.

Johnson, L.A. (1995). "Forum on Feminism and the Media: Afterword." *Signs* 20, no. 3: 711–719.

Kadi, J. (1996). *Thinking Class: Sketches from a Cultural Worker.* Boston: South End Press.

Kearney, M.C. (1998). "'Don't Need You': Rethinking Identity Politics and Separatism from a Grrl Perspective." In J. Epstein, ed., *Identity in a Postmodern World*, 148–183. Malden, MA: Blackwell.

Kitch, C. (2003). "Generational Memory and Identity in American News Magazines." *Journalism* 4, no. 2: 185–202.

Klanac, B. (2007, April 16). "Gazette on Notice as 'Spoof' Denounced." *Western News.* Retrieved 17 April 2007 from http://communications.uwo.ca/western_news/story.html?listing_id=23096.

Klein, M. (1997). "Duality and Redefinition: Young Feminism and the Alternative Music Community." In L. Heywood and J. Drake, eds., *Third Wave Agenda: Being Feminist, Doing Feminism*, 207–226. Minneapolis: University of Minnesota Press.

Klein, N. (1999). *No Logo: Taking Aim at the Brand Bullies.* Toronto: Knopf Canada.

Lamm, N. (2001). "It's a Big Fat Revolution." In. B. Findlen, ed., *Listen Up! Voices from the Next Feminist Generation*, 85–94. Seattle: Seal Press.

Lather, P. (1986). "Research as Praxis." *Harvard Educational Review* 56: 257–277.

REFERENCES

———. (1991). *Getting Smart: Feminist Research and Pedagogy with/in the Postmodern.* New York: Routledge.

———. (1992). "Critical Frames in Educational Research: Feminist and Poststructuralist Perspectives." *Theory into Practice* 21, no. 2: 87–99.

———. (2004). "Critical Inquiry in Qualitative Research: Feminist and Poststructuralist Perspectives: Science 'After Truth.'" In K. deMarrais and S.D. Lapan, eds., *Foundations of Research: Methods of Inquiry in Education and the Social Sciences*, 203–216. Mahwah, NJ: Lawrence Erlbaum Associates.

Lee, J.Y. (1995). "Beyond Bean Counting." In B. Findlen, ed., *Listen Up! Voices from the Next Feminist Generation*, 205–211. Seattle: Seal Press.

Levy, A. (2005). *Female Chauvinist Pigs: Women and the Rise of Raunch Culture.* New York: Free Press.

Lind, R.A., and C. Salo. (2002). "The Framing of Feminists and Feminism in News and Public Affairs Programs in U.S. Electronic Media." *Journal of Communication* 52, no. 1: 211–228.

Looser, D. (1997). "Introduction 2: Gen X Feminists? Youthism, Careerism and the Third Wave." In D. Looser and E.A. Kaplan, eds., *Generations: Academic Feminists in Dialogue*, 31–54. Minneapolis: University of Minnesota Press.

Looser, D., and E.A. Kaplan. (1997). "Preface." In D. Looser and E.A. Kaplan, eds., *Generations: Academic Feminists in Dialogue*, ix–xii. Minneapolis: University of Minnesota Press.

Lorde, A. (1984). *Sister/ Outsider: Essays and Speeches.* Berkeley: The Crossing Press.

Lubaton, V., and D. Lundy Martin. (2004). "Introduction: Making What We Will Become." In V. Lubaton and D. Lundy Martin, eds., *The Fire This Time: Young Activists and the New Feminism*, xxi–xxxvii. New York: Anchor.

Lugones, M.C., and E.V. Spelman. (1983). "Have We Got a Theory for You! Feminist Theory, Cultural Imperialism and the Demand for 'the Women's Voice.'" *Women's Studies International Forum* 6, no. 6: 573–581.

May, E. (2006). *How to Save the World in Your Spare Time.* Toronto: Key Porter.

Maynard, M. (2004). *Dress and Globalization.* Manchester: Manchester University Press.

Miller, M. (2007). "Coming of Age: The Fight for an All-inclusive Gender Studies Curriculum." *Our Schools / Our Selves* 17, no. 1: 85–92.

———. (2008). "It's Time to Take the Teaching Gender Aptitude Quiz!" *Our Schools / Our Selves* 17, no. 2: 123–132.

Mills, C. (2006, February/March). "Nuthin' but a G Thang." *London City Life*, 24–27.

Mills, S. (2003). "Third Wave Feminist Linguistics and the Analysis of Sexism." Retrieved 17 March 2007 from http://extra.shu.ac.uk/daol/articles/

closed/2003/001/mills2003001-paper.html.

Miss G__ Project for Equity in Education. (2005). "Informational Brochure." London, ON: Miss G__ Project.

—. (2006a). "The Miss G__ Chapters Manual." London, ON: Miss G__ Project.

—. (2006b, April 7). "Young Feminists Demand Women's Studies." Retrieved 20 January 2007 from http://rabble.ca/news_full_story.shtml?x=48961.htm.

—. (2007a). "The Miss G__ Project." Retrieved 12 April 2007 from www.themissgproject.org.

—. (2007b). "The Story of Miss G__." Retrieved 12 April 2007 from www.themissgproject.org/about/missg.html.

—. (2007c). "Everything You Wanted to Know about Women's and Gender Studies in High Schools." Retrieved 20 April 2007 from www.themissgproject.org/about/wgs.html#4.

Mitchell, A., L.B. Rundle, and L. Karaian, eds. (2001). *Turbo Chicks: Talking Young Feminisms*. Toronto: Sumach Press.

Mitchell, L. (2006, Summer). "The Next Generation of Feminists." *The Huron University College Grapevine*, 21–29.

Morgan, D. (1995). "Invisible Women: Young Women and Feminism." In G. Griffin, ed., *Feminist Activism in the 1990s*, 127–135. London: Taylor and Francis.

Morgan, R. (2003a). "Introduction: New World Women." In R. Morgan, ed., *Sisterhood Is Forever: The Women's Anthology for a New Millennium*, xv–lv. New York: Washington Square.

—. (2003b). "To Vintage Feminists." In R. Morgan, ed., *Sisterhood Is Forever: The Women's Anthology for a New Millennium*, 571–575. New York: Washington Square.

—. (2003c). "To Younger Women." In R. Morgan, ed., *Sisterhood Is Forever: The Women's Anthology for a New Millennium*, 576–580. New York: Washington Square.

Naples, N.A. (1999). "Towards Comparative Analyses of Women's Political Praxis: Explicating Multiple Dimensions of Standpoint Epistemology for Feminist Ethnography." *Women and Politics* 20, no. 1: 29–54.

—. (2003). *Feminism and Method: Ethnography, Discourse Analysis, and Activist Research*. New York: Routledge.

Newman, J., and L.A. White. (2006). *Women, Politics and Public Policy: The Political Struggles of Canadian Women*. Don Mills, ON: Oxford University Press.

No Doubt. (2003). "Just a Girl." *The Singles, 1992–2003*. [CD]. Santa Monica, CA: Intersound Records.

Norris, P. (1997). "Introduction." In P. Norris, ed., *Women, Media and Politics*,

REFERENCES

1–18. Cambridge: University of Oxford Press.

Oakley, A. (1981). "Interviewing Women: A Contradiction in Terms." In H. Roberts, ed., *Doing Feminist Research*, 30–61. London: Routledge and Kegan Paul.

Olson, A. (2006). "Womyn Before." In M. Berger, ed., *We Don't Need Another Wave: Dispatches from the Next Generation of Feminists*, 8–12. Emeryville, CA: Seal Press.

O'Neal, G.S. (1999). "The Power of Style: On Rejection of the Accepted." In K.P. Johnston and S.J. Lennon, eds., *Appearance and Power*, 127–140. New York: Oxford University Press.

Onion, R. (2006, Fall). "Tree So Horny: Can Sex Sell Environmentalism?" *Bitch: Feminist Response to Pop Culture* 33: 29–31.

Orr, C.M. (1997). "Charting the Currents of the Third Wave." *Hypatia* 12, no. 3: 29–45.

Parkins, W. (2002). *Fashioning the Body Politic: Dress, Gender, Citizenship*. New York: Oxford University Press.

Purvis, J. (2004). "Grrls and Women Together in the Third Wave: Embracing the Challenges of Intergenerational Feminism(s). *NWSA Journal* 16, no. 3: 93–123.

Rawlings, A. (2006). *Wide Slumber for Lepidopterists*. Toronto: Coach House Books.

"Read-In Boosts Bid for Women's Studies Credit." (2006, June 8). *Toronto Star*, R09. Retrieved 12 January 2007 from Proquest Canadian Newsstand database, available online from https://rsvpn.ubc.ca/http/proquest.umi.com.

Rebick, J. (2005). *Ten Thousand Roses: The Making of a Feminist Revolution*. Toronto: Penguin.

Rebick, J., and K. Roach. (1996). *Politically Speaking*. Vancouver: Douglas and McIntyre.

Reinharz, S. (1992). *Feminist Methods in Social Research*. New York: Oxford University Press.

Rhode, D. (1995). "Media Images, Feminist Issues." *Signs* 20, no. 3: 685–709.

Rich, A. (1986). "Disobedience and Women's Studies." In *Blood, Bread and Poetry: Selected Prose 1979–1985*, 76–84. New York: W.W. Norton.

—. (1979). *On Lies, Secrets and Silences: Selected Prose 1966–1978*. London: W.W. Norton.

Riordan, E. (2001). "Commodified Agents and Empowered Girls: Consuming and Producing Feminism." *Journal of Communication Inquiry* 25: 279–297.

Rivers, C. (1996). *Slick Spins and Fractured Facts: How Cultural Myths Distort the News*. New York: Columbia University Press.

Roiphe, K. (1994). *The Morning After: Fear, Sex and Feminism*. Boston: Back Bay Books.

Ross, B., and J. Dixon. (1958). "Lollipop" [Recorded by the Chordettes]. *Lollipop* [LP]. New York: Cadence/Columbia.

Ross, K. (2004). "Women Framed: The Gendered Turn in Mediated Politics." In K. Ross and C.M. Byerly, eds., *Women and Media: International Perspectives,* 60–80. Malden, MA: Blackwell.

Rubinstein, R.P. (2001). *Dress Codes: Meanings and Messages in American Culture.* 2nd ed. Boulder, CO: Westview Press.

Rundle, L.B. (1998, Fall). "Make Room Sister: The Next Generation is Here." *Herizons* 24, no. 27: 24.

Ryan, B. (1992). *Feminism and the Women's Movement: Dynamics of Change in Social Movement Ideology and Activism.* New York: Routledge.

Savoie, K. (2006). "Unnatural Selection: Questioning Science's Gender Bias." In L. Jervis and A. Zeisler, eds., *Bitchfest: Ten Years of Cultural Criticism from the Pages of Bitch Magazine,* 134–143. New York: Ferrar, Straus and Giroux.

School Community Safety Advisory Panel. (2008). *Final Report on School Safety.* Toronto: SCSAP.

Schroeder, P. (2003). "Running for Our Lives: Electoral Politics." In R. Morgan, ed., *Sisterhood Is Forever: The Women's Anthology for the New Millennium,* 28–42. New York: Washington Square.

Seely, M. (2007). *Fight Like a Girl: How To Be a Fearless Feminist.* New York: New York University Press.

Shulman, A.K. (1991). "Dances with Feminists." *Women's Review of Books* 9, no. 3. Retrieved 21 April 2007 from http://sunsite3.berkeley.edu/Goldman/Features/dances_shulman.htm.

Steenbergen, C. (1999). "Taking the 'Post' Off of Feminism: History, Sexuality, and the Politics of the Women's Movement's Third Wave." MA thesis, Carleton University, Ottawa.

—. (2001). "Feminism and Young Women: Alive and Well and Still Kicking." *Canadian Woman Studies/les cahiers de la femme* 20/21: 6–14.

Steinem, G. (1995a). "Foreword." In R. Walker, ed., *To Be Real: Telling the Truth and Changing the Face of Feminism,* xiii–xxviii. New York: Anchor.

—. (1995b). *Outrageous Acts and Everyday Rebellions.* 2nd ed. New York: Owl Books.

—. (2003). "The Media and the Movement: A User's Guide." In R. Morgan, ed., *Sisterhood Is Forever: The Women's Anthology for a New Millennium,* 103–120. New York: Washington Square.

Steiner, L. (1992). "The History and Structure of Women's Alternative Media." In L.F. Rakow, ed., *Women Making Meaning: New Feminist Directions in Communication,* 121–143. New York: Routledge.

Thompson, R. (2006). "Reading, Writing and Revolution on Miss G Lesson Plan."

REFERENCES

Herizons 20, no. 2: 7.

Thatcher Ulrich, L. (2007). *Well-Behaved Women Seldom Make History*. New York: Alfred A. Knopf.

Tucker, M. (2005, September 22). "High School Women's Studies the Goal of Miss G__ Project." *The Gazette* (University of Western Ontario). Retrieved 28 January 2007 from www.gazette.uwo.ca/article.cfm?section=FrontPage&articleI D=393&month=9&day=22&year=2005.

University of Windsor Action Girls. (2006, May 31). "Miss G Project Feminist Read-In." Message posted to www.femilicious.com/actiongirls/noe/31.

"Up the revolution!" (2007, April 18). *The Guardian*. Retrieved 18 April 2007 from http://www.guardian.co.uk/gender/story/0,,2059641,00.htm.

Valenti, J. (2007). *Full Frontal Feminism: A Young Woman's Guide to Why Feminism Matters*. Berkeley: Seal Press.

van Zoonen, L.A. (1992). "The Women's Movement and the Media: Constructing a Public Identity." *European Journal of Communication* 7: 453–476.

Walker, R. (1995). "To Be Real: An Introduction." In R. Walker, ed., *To Be Real: Telling the Truth and Changing the Face of Feminism*, xxix–xl. New York: Anchor.

Wells, J. (2005, July 23). "Case of Miss G Inspires Project." *Toronto Star*, L01. Retrieved 12 January 2007 from Proquest Canadian Newsstand database, available online from https://rsvpn.ubc.ca/http/proquest.umi.com.

Wetter, E. (2006, Fall). "My Body, My ... Gardenburger?" *Bitch: Feminist Response to Pop Culture* 34: 15.

Whittall, Z. (2006, June 8–14). "They Call Me Miss G: Queen's Park Read-In Makes Poetic Push for Women's Studies in High School." *NOW* Magazine. Retrieved 28 February 2007 from http://nowtoronto.com/issues/2006-06-08/news_story5.php.

Williams, A. (2006). "A Gap in the Movement." *This Magazine* 39(5): 18–20. Retrieved 29 September 2006 from Proquest Research Library, available online from https://rsvpn.ubc.ca/http/proquest.umi.com.

Wilson, E. (1985). *Adorned in Dreams: Fashion and Modernity*. London: Virago.

Wilson, J.K. (2001). *How the Left Can Win Arguments and Influence People: A Tactical Manual for Pragmatic Progressives*. New York: New York University Press.

Wrekk, A. (2003). *Stolen Sharpie Revolution: A DIY Zine Resource*. San Francisco: Microcosm.

Yukman, L. (1997). "Feminism and a Discontent." In L. Heywood and J. Drake, eds., *Third Wave Agenda: Being Feminist, Doing Feminism*, 168–177. Minneapolis: University of Minnesota Press.

INDEX

ability/disability issues, 17, 33, 77, 146
anti-feminism, 15–16, 101, 141

backlash against feminism, 15, 20, 21, 24, 28, 29, 31, 36, 50, 62, 66, 70–73, 79, 85, 87, 100, 104–105, 136–137, 146
Barnard, Malcolm, 51–52
Bartky, Sandra Lee, 51
Baumgardner, Jennifer, 14, 27, 29–30, 51, 67, 87
beauty culture: critique of, 43, 61, 70, 81
Birth of Feminism, The, 103
Bitch magazine, 25
"blackout as social control," 59
bluestockings, 41, 95, 96, 97–98, 137
blogs, 14, 19, 68, 151, 152, 153, 159, 162. *See also* technology
Bordo, Susan, 51, 70–73
Bourdieu, Pierre, 75
bra-burning, as caricatures of feminists, 59–60. *See also* feminists
branding, 21, 24, 36, 82. *See also* feminism, for sale; Miss G__ Project
Briarpatch, 15, 151, 153
Bronstein, Carolyn, 56, 58, 62, 125
Brown, Louise, 39, 124–127, 136–137. *See also Toronto Star*

Canadian Woman Studies, 14
capital: cultural, 53, 56, 75–76; social, 56, 75–76, 80, 101, 111, 124. *See also* social class
capitalism, and neoliberalism 23, 24, 27, 50, 57, 67, 82, 132–133, 150. *See also* feminism, for sale
CBC Radio, 123, 124, 160
Cho, Margaret, 16, 90
CityTV, 39
class issues, 17, 33, 45, 137, 145. *See also* social class
Cole, Susan G., 29
Corcoran, Terence, 60
Coulter, Rebecca, 28, 128, 154

depoliticization of goals, 13, 22–23, 37, 100–101, 105–106, 114, 115, 162.
DiFranco, Ani, 42, 52, 85, 86

do it yourself (DIY), 14, 143, 153
docile bodies, 43, 51, 70–73
dress, semiotics, 51, 93, 95–99; social importance of, 37, 51, 93–99
Dubinsky, Kate, 130–131
dutiful daughters, 23, 111–113, 114, 165
Dworkin, Andrea, 102

Facebook, 152, 157, 159, 162. *See also* technology
Falconer Report, 152, 163, 174
femininity: 12, 13, 21, 37, 43, 50–51, 54, 56, 61, 62, 63, 65–73, 76, 81, 86, 87, 91, 96, 99, 100, 106–110, 126, 134, 135, 166
feminism: coming to 29–30; as "the f word," 30, 50, 56, 100, 103, 143, 144; and fashion, 23, 24; for sale, 23, 82, 133, 154; identification of, 103–104, 106–107; liberal, 22; packaging of, 106–110; post-feminism, 15, 16; and the public imagination 47, 50, 55, 59, 71, 95, 97, 99, 104, 147, 156; as transformational, 22–23, 28, 105, 145–146, 148, 156
"feminism is dead," 15–16, 59
feminism lite: as media frame, 51, 58, 62–63, 125, 127, 131, 136, 149
feminism, waves of, 18, 24–26, 31–33, 66–67, 69–70, 102, 112, 164; and coalition building, 66, 146, 147, 153, 162, 165; conflict between, 20, 27, 47, 58, 62–63, 66, 146; informed criticisms of, 16, 31–33, 47, 109, 165. *See also* first wave, second wave, third wave
"feminist insecurity," 17. *See also* third wave
feministing.org, 19, 68
feminists: caricatures of, 21, 31, 36, 50, 60, 62, 63, 70, 104, 162; heterosexual, 56, 67, 68, 87, 96; lesbian, 21–22, 31, 50–51, 79, 87–88, 104, 162; as sexy, 56, 65, 69, 97, 102–103
Final Report on School Safety. See Falconer Report
first wave, 24, 25, 27. *See also* feminism, waves of
Foucault, Michel, 51, 70

· 188

INDEX·

Freeman, Barbara, 14, 15, 54, 60
Friedan, Betty, 102
Full Frontal Feminism, 19, 68

Gazette, The, 127–130, 141, 162; and "Labia Majora Carnage," 158–160. *See also* University of Western Ontario
gender: construction and socialization of, 12; identity, 32, 65, 96; injustice/oppression, 26, 45, 95; performativity, 36, 66, 68, 80–81, 94, 127; and relationships, 48
gender-based violence. *See* violence against women
Gendering the Vertical Mosaic, 15
Ghabrial, Sarah: 12, 35, 39, 44–46, 49, 74, 83, 100, 114, 124, 131–133, 137, 139–140, 145, 147, 149, 165
"girlie": 36, 43, 50–51, 61, 66–70, 72–76, 81, 98, 126, 164, 165, 166. *See also* media strategy, femininity
Girls Gone Wild, 88
Gitlin, Todd, 57
Globe and Mail, 60
Goldman, Emma, 80
Grady, Lora, 154
grassroots activism, 74, 140, 152, 154
The Guardian, 68
Guerilla Girls, 103

Hamilton, Roberta, 15
Hanna, Kathleen, 133
Herizons, 14, 37, 42, 124, 143–144, 147, 148, 153
homophobia, 22, 31, 33, 44, 45, 50, 68–69, 88, 89–90, 112, 128, 158–160; anti-homophobia, 22, 51, 87, 90
hooks, bell, 17, 26, 28, 32, 69, 95, 135–136, 166
Hurdis, Rebecca, 79
Huron Grapevine, The, 53, 141–143, 147, 148. *See also* University of Western Ontario

identity politics, 32, 73–74, 76–80, 98
"I'm not a feminist, but," 100, 107

Jervis, Lisa, 25, 26, 50, 114

Karaian, Lara, 14

Kennedy, Flo, 103
Kennedy, Gerard, 40, 99, 136
Klein, Naomi, 68

Lee, JeeYuen, 77–78
lesbian continuum, 89
lobbying strategies: 20, 35, 36, 39-44, 46-48, 72, 74, 81, 109–110, 111, 123, 127, 135, 136, 148, 149–150, 152, 155, 156, 157, 162, 164, 166. *See also* "New Girls' Club Luncheon," No More Miss Nice G__, postcard campaign, Read-In
London City Life, 134–135, 147
London Free Press, 130–133, 147

MacLean's magazine, 60
Manifesta, 14, 68, 72
May, Elizabeth, 108–109
McClung's magazine, 124, 154
media, feminist: 37, 47, 124, 141–148, 150, 151, 152, 153–155, 161–162
media images: cheekiness, 11, 127, 152, 158; girl group, 46, 125, 132, 149; "good-time girls," 12–13, 73, 98–99, 125, 129, 137, 138, 152, 163–164, 167; humorous, 94, 152; intelligent, 12–13, 128, 144, 147, 152, 160–161, 163; reappropriation of, 41, 43, 84, 94
media, mainstream: 21, 37, 39, 48, 59, 101, 124, 133, 137, 148–150, 151, 153, 154–155, 161, 162, 167; delegitimization frame, 36, 47, 54, 56, 60, 62, 99, 115, 127, 129, 136, 140–142, 144, 149; demonization frame, 31, 36, 50, 54, 56, 60–62, 150; feminism lite frame, 51, 58, 62–63, 125, 127, 131, 136, 149; and manipulation, 31, 36; marginalization frame, 36, 53, 56, 57, 58–60, 61, 139, 149; polarization of issues, 58, 62, 146; and relationships with feminists, 14, 52–53, 55, 57, 64, 91–92, 102, 105, 123; trivialization of issues, 31, 36, 53, 56, 57, 63, 130–131, 140
media strategy: 35, 110, 157, 158–160, 164; apolitical, 12–13, 21, 37, 55–56, 105–106, 108, 112, 162; and femininity, 12, 37, 50, 56, 72–73, 82, 86, 96–100, 125, 126, 129, 137, 138, 157, 162, 164, 166–167; "feminism"

189·

and strategic deployment of, 37, 56, 91, 100–101, 104–106, 108, 131; heterosexualization, 22, 56, 82, 88-90, 96, 128–130, 157; media darling, 123, 133, 161; and media savvy, 56, 123–124, 155; "playing the game": 23, 37, 76, 110–111, 113–114, 128, 132, 167; subversion containment: 132; Trojan Containment, 12–13, 99, 162
middle class, 20, 31, 75, 79, 80, 109–110
Mills, Cyndi, 135
"Miss Education," 41, 95, 96–99, 137
Miss G__, identity of: 12, 44–45, 85, 123, 125, 138–139
Miss G__ Project: chapters: 17, 33, 48; Chapter Manual, 33, 48, 49; critiques of, 16, 28, 30–31, 47, 109, 165–166; goals of, 17, 35, 37, 48, 85, 88, 96, 115, 167; leadership, 35–36, 138; logo of, 12, 23, 36, 82, 83–85, 125, 128, 132, 163; mandate of, 17, 22, 44, 46, 48, 112, 153, 166; and marketing 21, 23, 82, 91, 100, 132; networking, 20, 27, 39–40, 111, 123, 139, 153, 161, 166; and public imagination, 156; steering committee of, 12, 17, 21, 35, 46, 69, 73, 81, 113–114, 138, 143, 165; as watchdog organization, 166; website of, 143, 151, 157; and women's studies curriculum, 166; workshops of, 48, 49, 75, 80, 131, 149, 150, 166. *See also* lobbying strategies, media images, media strategies, supporters
Mitchell, Alyson, 14
Mitchell, Laurel, 124, 140–143, 148, 159–160, 165
Mohan, Dilani, 12, 30, 35, 43, 46, 49, 74, 78, 81, 82–83, 86, 97, 101–102, 109, 123, 127, 132, 145, 165
Morgan, Debi, 15
Morgan, Robin, 15, 26, 30, 147

Naples, Nancy, 17, 22, 34
National Action Committee (NAC), 72–73
National Organization of Women (NOW), 53, 60
Neoliberalism, 23, 28, 66, 82
"New Girls' Club Luncheon," 36, 39–41, 76, 91, 96–99, 112, 136–137, 151, 161, 167. See also lobbying strategies

No More Miss Nice G__! 152, 163, 169–176. *See also* lobbying strategies
NOW magazine, 37, 42, 43, 139–141, 144
Old Boys' Club, 40–41, 96, 97, 98
"Old Girls," 41
Olson, Alix, 30
Ontario: education system of, 11, 16, 85; educational policy of, 16–17; legislative assembly of, 40; ministry of education, 11, 153, 171–177
oppression, intersectionality of, 11, 17, 26, 32–33, 77, 135, 137, 145–146, 152, 154, 161
Our Schools/Our Selves, 124, 153
Owsianik, Jenna, 147, 152, 159, 163–164, 165, 169–176

People for the Ethical Treatment of Animals (PETA), 131, 133
postcard campaign, 11–12, 152. *See also* lobbying strategies
postmodernism, 25, 28, 47, 65, 77, 94
praxis, 19, 35
public imagination: and feminism, 47, 50, 55, 59, 71, 95, 97, 99, 104, 147, 156
Pupatello, Sandra, 40, 42, 113, 138, 140, 142

Queen's Park,12, 39–44, 75, 80, 91, 96, 111, 136–137, 155
queer issues, 32, 43, 65, 68–70, 87, 96, 112, 137, 139, 146, 158, 160

race issues, 17, 22, 33, 45, 69, 74, 76–80, 84, 107–108, 109, 110, 134, 135, 137, 145, 146, 161; and tokenism, 78, 110
raunch culture, 69, 88, 145
Rawal, Sheetal: 12, 30, 35, 44–46, 48, 49, 73, 74, 75, 78, 81, 82, 86, 88–89, 101–102, 128, 130, 131–132, 134, 135, 140, 142, 147, 148, 149, 162, 165, 170–171
Read-In, 36, 42–44, 111–112, 137–145, 155, 167. *See also* lobbying strategies
Rebick, Judy, 15, 28, 32, 39, 42, 52, 53, 54, 56, 58, 114, 141–142, 150, 155
research, insider, 33–35
Rich, Adrienne, 23, 89, 137
Richards, Amy, 14, 27, 29–30, 51, 67
riot grrls, 43
Roach, Kiki, 15, 32, 52, 53, 54, 56, 58, 114, 150, 154

INDEX

Royal Commission on the Status of Women, 54
Rundle, Lisa, Bryn, 14, 15
second wave: 14, 20, 21, 24, 25, 27, 28–29, 32, 46, 58, 62–63, 67, 69–71, 72, 77–80, 94, 102, 112, 146, 161. *See also* feminism, waves of
Seely, Megan, 62, 76
sexism, 17, 22, 29, 44, 128
sexual harassment, 23, 158, 174
sexuality issues, 17, 32, 48, 68–72, 77, 87, 107, 137
Shameless magazine, 14, 37, 42, 48, 53, 124, 144–148, 153, 160
Shdorkoff, Lara, 12, 21, 46, 49, 73, 75, 78, 80–81, 82, 83, 86, 88–89, 97, 101, 103, 123, 125, 129–132, 135, 137, 138, 165
sidebar history, 105, 145
social class, 22, 53, 69, 73–75, 78, 96, 98, 100–101, 107–108, 110–111, 135, 161
Steinem, Gloria, 15, 29, 71, 102, 154, 155
Steyn, Mark, 60–61
structural inequality, 32, 105
supporters: 12, 39, 80, 136, 159–160; conservative, 22, 40, 43, 89, 101–102, 109, 111–112, 146, 167; male, 49, 98–99, 111–112, 140, 145; non-feminist, 52; superficial, 99, 100, 146, 149, 167

T-shirts: for Miss G__ Project, 23, 36, 49, 74, 82, 83–86, 90, 95, 125, 134, 138, 139, 147; "This Is What a Feminist Looks Like," 44, 86, 90, 138, 139
technology, 26, 27, 151–153, 164, 175. *See also* blogs, Facebook, YouTube
Ten Thousand Roses, 39, 42
Thirdspace, 153
third wave, 13, 16, 24, 25, 28–29, 36, 46, 50, 72, 73, 76, 88, 90, 94, 102, 110, 112–113, 164–165; body politic: 67–68; as "Do-me" feminism: 31, 51, 63, 67; as feminism lite, 51, 58; messiness/hybridity of, 18, 65–66, 69; multiplicity/pluralism of, 32, 33, 65–66, 69, 77–80, 87, 95, 146; and negative attention, 17, 18, 20, 27, 31, 67–68, 103; personal narrative/anthologies of, 14–15, 18, 77; as superficial: 63, 67–68, 103; and technology, 26, 27, 151. *See also* feminism, waves of
Third Wave Agenda, 15

This Bridge Called My Back, 79. *See also* race issues
This Magazine, 153
Toronto Star, 37, 39, 41, 42, 43–44, 91, 97, 98, 102, 103, 115, 123, 124–127, 130, 135–139, 144, 149, 151, 155, 160, 164
Trojan Containment, 12–13, 99, 162. *See also* media strategy
Turbo Chicks, 14

University of Western Ontario, 44–45, 53, 123; and chilly climate, 159; Huron College, 44

Valenti, Jessica: 19, 68–69, 87, 90
Valentine's Day Phone-In, 163–164: script of, 169–176
Violence against women, 12, 23, 139, 160, 163

Walker, Rebecca, 14
Well-Behaved Women Rarely Make History, 24
Wells, Jennifer, 103, 124–127
white supremacist capitalist patriarchy, 17, 28, 69, 95
whiteness, 69, 84, 109, 132, 134, 135, 157
Whittall, Zoe, 139–141
Whole World Is Watching, The, 57
Williams, Audra, 17, 77
Wolf, Naomi, 102
women's movement: history of, 15, 16, 17–19, 20, 21, 22, 25, 36, 45, 48, 54, 59, 66, 69, 79, 85, 94–96, 98, 105, 138, 164
women's studies/women's and gender studies, 11, 17, 19, 20, 24, 42, 45–46, 48, 52, 90, 97, 99, 104–106, 108, 113–114, 127, 129, 132, 138, 140–142, 145, 152, 153, 157, 164, 166, 173–174; as apolitical, 13, 22, 100, 101, 105, 114, 155–156; "for girls only," 49, 136–137, 142
working class, 22, 69, 74–76
Wynne, Kathleen, 42, 101, 111, 113, 138, 163, 172–174

young people: as apathetic, 15
YouTube, 152, 163,

zines, 14, 19, 68, 151, 153

191

Other Titles from The Women's Issues Publishing Program

D is for Daring: The Women behind the Films of Studio D
Gail Vanstone

Trans/forming Feminisms: Transfeminist Voices Speak Out
Edited by Krista Scott-Dixon

Remembering Women Murdered by Men: Memorials Across Canada
The Cultural Memory Group

Growing up Degrassi: Television, Identity and Youth Cultures
Edited by Michele Byers

Feminism, Law, Inclusion: Intersectionality in Action
Edited by Gayle MacDonald, Rachel L. Osborne and Charles C. Smith

Troubling Women's Studies: Pasts, Presents and Possibilities
Ann Braithwaite, Susan Heald, Susanne Luhmann and Sharon Rosenberg

Doing IT: Women Working in Information Technology
Krista Scott-Dixon

Inside Corporate U: Women in the Academy Speak Out
Edited by Marilee Reimer

Out of the Ivory Tower: Feminist Research for Social Change
Edited by Andrea Martinez and Meryn Stuart

Strong Women Stories: Native Vision and Community Survival
Edited by Kim Anderson and Bonita Lawrence

Back to the Drawing Board: African-Canadian Feminisms
Edited by Njoki Nathane Wane, Katerina Deliovsky and Erica Lawson

Cashing In On Pay Equity? Supermarket Restructuring and Gender Equality
Jan Kainer

Double Jeopardy: Motherwork and the Law
Lorna A. Turnbull

Turbo Chicks: Talking Young Feminisms
Edited by Allyson Mitchell, Lisa Bryn Rundle and Lara Karaian

Women in the Office: Transitions in a Global Economy
Ann Eyerman

Women's Bodies/Women's Lives: Women, Health and Well-Being
Edited by Baukje Miedema, Janet Stoppard and Vivienne Anderson

A Recognition of Being: Reconstructing Native Womanhood
Kim Anderson

Women's Changing Landscapes: Life Stories from Three Generations
Edited by Greta Hofmann Nemiroff

Women Working the NAFTA Food Chain: Women, Food and Globalization
Edited by Deborah Barndt

Cracking the Gender Code: Who Rules the Wired World?
Melanie Stewart Millar

Redefining Motherhood: Changing Identities and Patterns
Edited by Sharon Abbey and Andrea O'Reilly

Fault Lines: Incest, Sexuality and Catholic Family Culture
Tish Langlois